EXPORTING
TO
SCANDINAVIA
including Denmark, Finland, Iceland, Norway and Sweden

EXPORTING
TO
SCANDINAVIA

including Denmark, Finland, Iceland, Norway and Sweden

CONSULTANT EDITORS:
Gerry O'Brien
and Adam Jolly

in association with

Department of Trade and Industry

SCANDINAVIAN AIRLINES

KOGAN
PAGE

First published in 1998

Kogan Page Limited
120 Pentonville Road
London N1 9JN

© Kogan Page and contributors, 1998

British Library Cataloguing in Publication Data

ISBN 0 7494 2691 8

Department of Trade and Industry URN 98/776

Typeset by JS Typesetting, Wellingborough, Northants.
Printed and bound by Bell and Bain Ltd., Glasgow

Pure Scandinavian

A FLYING START TO BUSINESS IN SCANDINAVIA

Flying to Scandinavia on business? Then choose the airline that gives you an excellent choice of departures to 7 major Scandinavian cities.

From Heathrow, for example, you can choose from any of our 5 non-stop flights a day to Copenhagen, Oslo or Stockholm – or from our twice daily non-stop services both to Gothenburg and Stavanger.

SAS also offers excellent non-stop and connecting services to Scandinavia from Stansted, Manchester, Aberdeen and Dublin.

For flight details and bookings call your travel agent or SAS on 0845 60 727 727.

Internet: http://www.sas.se

SCANDINAVIAN AIRLINES

Contents

Contributor Details

Rob Allaker is the International Marketing Executive with CDDC, the Inward Investment and Trade Development arm of Durham County Council. His work involves regular travel to Finland and he has organised a number of trade missions and events, often in partnership with the DTI Finland Desk and Embassy in Helsinki.

Rob Allaker
International Marketing Executive
County Durham Development Company
County Hall
Durham DH1 5UT
UK
Tel: +44 (0)191 383 2000
Fax: +44 (0)191 386 2974
e-mail: rob@cddc.co.uk
web site: http://www.cddc.co.uk

Harley Atherton
T F Marketing is an organisation specialising in working in the UK as one of the partners for INTERPRISE events, particularly those in Scandinavia. For more information contact T F Marketing on:

Tel: +44 (0)1636 830995
Fax: +44 (0)1636 830996
E Mail: tfmarket@msn.com

Laura Black is a consultant for Euro PA & Associates. Euro PA was awarded the British Consultant's Bureau's 'Small Consultancy of the Year' in November 1997.

Euro PA & Associates
Head Office
11 Church St
Northborough
Cambs, PE6 9BN
UK
Tel: +44 (0)1733 253006
Fax: +44 (0)1733 252489
Email: euro-pa@euro-pa.demon.co.uk
Web: www.euro-pa.co.uk

London Office
The Base
122 Brompton Road
Knightsbridge
London SW3 1JE
UK
Tel: +44 (0)171 591 4709
Fax: +44 (0)171 591 4705

Mr. Martin Börresen is a partner of Lagerlöf & Leman Advokatbyrå. He is practising in the areas of general commercial law, corporate law and competition law and is very well experienced in advising foreign clients doing business in Scandinavia.

Lagerlöf & Leman Advokatbyrå is one of Scandinavia's largest law firms with more than 100 lawyers. It provides legal advice concerning all types of business matters for both Swedish and foreign clients and has recently expanded its international presence by membership in the Alliance of European Lawyers, a close cooperation between six leading European law firms. The Alliance has joint offices in London, New York, Prague, Warsaw and Brussels, the latter providing specialised assistance in EU law matters.

Box 5402
Stockholm, SE-114 84
Sweden
Tel: +46 8665 6600
Fax: +46 8667 6883

Tom Burnham is the DTI Export Promoter for Scandinavia and the Nordic Countries. He can be contacted on:

Tel & Fax: +44 (0)1835 830758

Ole H. Christensen is a Commercial Officer at the British Embassy, Copenhagen. Previously he was employed at SKF Danmark as manager of Sales and Marketing of constructional steels and prior to that worked for Sandviken Group selling stainless and special steels. He has also worked as a Forwarding and Shipping agent.

A graduate of Copenhagen School of Commerce, Shipping and Forwarding, Mr Christensen has also followed courses in steel metallurgy and holds two degrees equivalent to Higher National Certificate in Business Administration ("MERKONOM" - Marketing and Export Marketing).

Robert Clark is Executive Director of Corporate Intelligence on Retailing.

Founded in 1987 by ex-Economist Intelligence Unit senior executives, Corporate Intelligence is Europe's foremost specialist provider of high quality, research-based information and analysis on UK and European retailing, retailers and consumer product markets. The formats in which they are presented include regular subscription services; market, country and topic reports; on-line services; and customised research and consultancy. Since 1995 Corporate Intelligence has been a joint venture partner of Lebhar-Friedman, Inc., North America's leading retail trade journal publisher.

48 Bedford Square
London WC1B 3DP
Tel: +44 (0)171 696 9006
Fax: +44 (0)171 696 9004

Christopher Cook is a Partner and Senior Trade Mark Attorney at Forrester Ketley & Co. which was established in 1884 and has substantial expertise in all areas of intellectual property, providing advice on securing Patent, Trade Mark, Design and Copyright protection in the UK and throughout the world. The firm has offices in London and Birmingham with associated firms in Germany and Eastern Europe.

Forrester Ketley & Co.
Forrester House
52 Bounds Green Road
London N11 2EY
UK
Tel: +44 (0)181 889 6622
Fax: +44 (0)181 881 1088
E Mail: foresters_lon@compuserve.com

DFDS Transport – Scandinavian Division.
The company is the prime specialist in multi-modal freight transportation and logistics services to and from the entire Scandinavian region, and offers a comprehensive service to all parts of the region, including Finland, as well as Denmark, Sweden and Norway. Services to Iceland are also available, either using direct container shipping links from Britain, or via Denmark.

DFDS Transport also has an extensive network of offices in the UK and Ireland and can offer regular services to all Nordic countries.

DFDS Transport Limited
Anglia Cargo Terminal
Coggeshall Bypass
Coggeshall
Essex CO6 1TL
UK
Tel: +44 (0)1376 565634
Fax: +44 (0)1376 565600

Distribution Projects Ltd. and **EP-Logistics Oy** specialise in logistics consultancy, and are able to provide advice on all aspects of supply chain planning. Neither company has any commercial arrangement with contractors, and their advice is therefore totally independent and objective.

Tony Elsom
Managing Director
Distribution Projects Ltd.
DPL House
2 Hunters Walk
Canal Street
Chester CH1 4EB
UK
Tel: +44 (0)1244 313283
Fax: +44 (0)1244 344704
Email: dpl@dproj.demon.co.uk

Jussi Jalanka
Managing Director
EP-Logistics Oy
Tehtaankatu 29A
FIN 00150
Helsinki
Finland

Tel: +358 9134 4531
Fax: +358 9134 45300
Email: Jussi.Jalanka@ep-logistics.fi

ECGD – The Export Credits Guarantee Department – is a Government Department, which promotes UK exports by insuring them against the risks of non-payment by overseas buyers. It also provides protection for UK companies investing overseas. ECGD is regulated by an Act of Parliament – the Export and Investment Guarantees Act 1991 – and is responsible to the President of the Board of Trade.

If you would like more information on any of ECGD's facilities, please contact the Help Desk on 0171 512 7887.

ECGD
PO Box 2200, 2 Exchange Tower
Harbour Exchange Square
London, E14 9GS
UK

Griffin Credit Services Limited
Farncombe Road
Worthing
BN11 2BW
UK
Tel: +44 (0)1903 205181
Fax: +44 (0)1903 214101

Griffin Credit Services Limited is a wholly-owned subsidiary of Midland Bank plc. Midland Bank is a wholly-owned subsidiary of HSBC Holdings plc which, with some 5,000 offices in 78 countries and territories, and assets of £275 billion at 30 June 1997, is one of the world's largest banking and financial services organisations.

Griffin Credit Services Limited is a holder of the Investors in People award and was the first business finance company to be a finalist in the UK's premier independent award in 1996: the British Quality Foundation (BQF) business excellence award.

Stefan S. Gudjonsson, cand oecon
The author is the Secretary General of the Federation of Icelandic Trade and is on the board of several Icelandic companies in trade and services. Mr. Gudjonsson is a business graduate from the University of Iceland. Prior to Univerisity Mr. Gudjonsson spent three years of study in London. Mr. Gudjonsson is the Honorary Consul of Bangladesh in Iceland.

The Federation of Icelandic Trade is a privately funded trade organisation representing companies in international trade, wholesaling and retail distribution. The organisation provides numerous services to its members including policy papers, education, trade information and business services.   (

Federation of Icelandic Trade
Kringlunni 7
103, Reykjavik
Iceland
Tel: +354 588 8910
Fax: +354 568 8441
E mail: fis@centrum.is

The Institute of Export was founded in 1935, with a mission to enhance the export performance of the UK by setting and raising professional standards in international trade management and export practice. It offers Education and Training, Specialised Business Information and also represents the views of its 6,000 members in export matters.

Aileen Prendergast
Information Department
Institute of Export
64 Clifton Street
London EC2
UK
Tel: +44 (0)171 247 9812
Fax: +44 (0)171 377 5343

The Institute of Management is a professional membership body whose mission is to promote the art and science of management through its management development programme and its research, publishing and information services. The material in this book is part of the *IM Management Checklists* which holds over 150 titles.

The Institute of Management
Management House
Cottingham Road
Corby
Northants NN17 1TT
UK
Tel: +44 (0)1536 204222
Fax: +44 (0)1536 201651

Manzoor G. K. Ishani is a senior partner with Mundays (solicitors) with offices in London, Brussels and Esher. He is a member of the Legal Committee of the British Franchise Association and co-author of 'Franchising in the UK', 'Franchising in Europe' and 'Franchising in Canada'. He has over 20 years' experience in assisting UK businesses to franchise in the UK and internationally in over 23 countries.

Mundays Solicitors
Hamilton House
Temple Avenue
London EC4Y 0HA
UK
Tel: +44 (0)171 437 8080
Fax: +44 (0)171 437 8180
Website http://www.lds.co.uk/franchise/legal/mundays

Dr Carl James is a Director of NJM Ltd and **Gonzalo Shoobridge** is a Consultant.

NJM Ltd provides consultancy in European affairs, innovation, technology transfer and economic development. The company has vast experience in potential external sources of finance for SMEs intending to internationalise their business strategies.

NJM Ltd
4 Church Lane
Pudsey
Leeds LS28 7BD
UK
Tel: +44 (0)113 236 1835
Fax: +44 (0)113 236 1284

Mark Johnson, principal assistant solicitor of the Infrastructure Group at SJ Berwin & Co, advises on major infrastructure projects and has extensive transactional experience in project finance and PFI in the United Kingdom and overseas. His areas of expertise range from transportation and energy, to healthcare, education and government office accommodation.

Mark Johnson
SJ Berwin & Co
222 Gray's Inn Road
London WC1X 8HB
UK
Tel: +44 (0)171 533 2222
Fax: +44 (0)171 533 2093
E-mail: mark.johnson@sjberwin.com

Finn Kern is the Director of the Danish Association of Advertising Agencies (DRB).

Danske Reklamebureauers Brancheforening (DRB)
Badstuestraede 20
PO Box 74
1003 Copenhagen K
Denmark
Tel: +45 3313 4444
Fax: +45 3311 6303
E-mail: drb@drb.dk
Website: www.drb.dk

Leaseurope is the European Federation of Equipment Leasing Company Associations and was founded in 1972. Members currently come from some 30 different countries, with about 1,500 leasing companies represented.

Leaseurope's day-to-day business is to inform leasing companies via their national associations of any change in taxation, accounting and other legislation in the early stages. Leaseurope's technical expertise is encapsulated in the different technical committees, which bring together respective national experts in the following areas: 'accounting and taxation', 'statistics and marketing', 'legal affairs', 'real estate leasing', 'car leasing' and 'Central and Eastern Europe'.

Leaseurope
Ave de Tervuren 267
B-1150 Brussels
Belgium
Tel: +32 2778 0560
Fax: +32 2778 0579

Karl Mackie is one of the Centre for Dispute Resolution's most experienced mediators having undertaken some of its most difficult cases including those which have pioneered the use of mediation in new sectors.

He is an Honorary Professor in ADR at the University of Birmingham Faculty of Law and has edited and authored several texts on ADR.

Centre for Dispute Resolution (CEDR)
3rd Floor, Princes House
95 Gresham Street
London EC2V 7NA
UK
Tel: +44 (0) 171 600 0500
Fax: +44 (0) 171 600 0501

Bob Mason is a business consultant, specialising in both the tele-communications sector and the Nordic markets. He is a former DTI Export Promoter for the Nordic region and is a regular presenter at the Centre for International Briefing at Farnham Castle. He may be contacted at:

REM Consultants
25 Sandringham Court
Pengwern Road
Shrewsbury
UK
SY3 8LL
Tel/Fax: +44 (0)1743 344948
E-mail: Rem@btinternet.com

Martin Morgan
International Business Manager
Lloyds Bank Plc
International Business, NW
Lloyds Bank Commercial Service
PO Box 349
4th Floor, Lloyds Bank Bdgs, 53 King St
Manchester, M60 2LE
UK
Tel: +44 (0)161 829 2936
Fax: +44 (0)161 8292968

Headquartered in Monaco, **Morgan & Partners** has offices in Sweden – Stockholm, Gothenburg and Malmo – and links throughout Scandinavia and the Nordic countries as well as offices in London and other major European cities. However, we have retained a boutique feel to our business, with a total of only 15 partners around Europe. For the last 15 years, we have been advising a variety of clients on European recruitment, and helping European candidates to make the best career choice. All our consultants have the linguistic and cultural understanding to enable them to give you the right advice if you are looking to make a cross-border move, either as an employee or an employer.

Jan Johnsson
Morgan & Partners
Bellmansgatan 8
118 20 Stockholm
Sweden
Tel: +46 8641 5760
Fax: +46 8643 2645
Website: www.morgan-partners.com
E-mail: jan.johnsson@morgan-partners.com

The Profi Group is a comprehensive property consultancy and has offices in all Nordic countries.

Head Office
The Profi Group
Norrlandsgatan 22, III
S 111 43 Stockholm
Sweden
Tel: +46 8440 3740
Fax: +46 8678 1523

Alan Ramby
Ramby and Partners, Copenhagen. Independent property consultants founded in 1980 and mainly focusing on international transactional and consultancy activities.

Ramby and Partners
Hoeghsmindevej 32
2820 Gentofte
Copenhagen
Denmark
Tel: +45 3976 0800
Fax: +45 3976 0810

Robert Rangecroft has a background in journalism, PR consultancy and corporate publishing and is a former Head of Publishing & Marketing at both the CBI and the London Stock Exchange. He is founder and joint managing director of London-based publishing services company RNP Limited, which has clients in Sweden including the Swedish Marketing Federation and the UK - industrial & commercial companies, national representative bodies, City & financial institutions and professional practices.

Robert Rangecroft
RNP Ltd
230 Great Guildford Business Square
30 Great Guildford Street
London, SEI 0HS
UK
Tel: +44 (0)171 620 0597
Fax: +44 (0)171 928 3386

Reino Routamo
Managing Director
Interdevelopment Oy

Born in 1931 in Helsinki, Mr. Routamo has been a professional management consultant since 1969 (member LJK/FEACO 1978) and since 1986 lived in Vienna, Austria, but continued to operate also from his Helsinki base. Working experience also in Finland, Sweden, Switzerland, Indonesia; professional visits to most European and North American countries, as well as to many developing countries in East Asia and Africa.

Specialist in strategic planning, international marketing and market studies, international investment promotion, training of consultants, training for feasibility studies; lecturer in foreign trade and international business development in Finnish Institute of Marketing.

Tel: +358 9241 2557 (Finland)
Fax: +358 9241 2558
Fax: +43 1512 3789 (Austria)

Clive Smithers
County Durham On Line is part of County Durham TEC, developing the Information Society for All in County Durham. It also leads or participates in a number of international research and development, service delivery and dissemination projects. It is currently developing a series of on line manuals for SMEs on electronic commerce.

For further information visit the website at
http://www.cdtec.co.uk

or e-mail to
enquiries@cdtec.co.uk

Clive Smithers
County Durham On Line
Unit 1B
Mountjoy Research Centre
Stockton Road
Durham DH1 3SW
UK
Tel: +44 (0)191 383 5000
Fax: +44 (0)191 383 5005

Oscar Sohl is Head of Public Procurement for the Ekero Kommun and a winner of a prize from the Swedish SOI for building up the Public Procurement Department at Ekero.

Oscar Sohl
Ekero Kommun
Tappstromsvagen 2
Ekero, S-178 23
Sweden
Tel: +46 8560 39110
Fax: +46 8560 35838

Nigel Swycher is a partner in the Intellectual Property Group of Slaughter and May.

Slaughter and May
35 Basinghall Street
London EC2V 5DB
UK
Tel: +44 (0)171 600 1200
Fax: +44 (0)171 726 0038
Website http://www.slaughterandmay.com

Kevin Thorne is an International Taxation Partner and **David White** a senior manger responsible for Growth & Development Services at Grant Thornton, a leading financial and business adviser to owner-managed businesses and their owners. It aims to help clients realise their ambitions locally, nationally and internationally via a network of 40 offices in the UK and an international network with representation in over 85 countries.

Grant Thornton
Grant Thornton House
Melton Street
Euston Square
London NW1 2EP
UK
Tel: +44 (0)171 383 5100
Fax: +44 (0)171 383 4715

Morten Tveten is a Partner in Montani AS. He has previously worked for Gemini Consulting and Bates in Norway as well as being a former Secretary General and Vice President of The Young European Federalists. He holds an MBA from Lausanne and a Master of Law from the University of Oslo.

Montani AS is a Norwegian-based business development and management agency, with special focus on the international oil and gas industry. Their core areas of involvement are strategy development, internationalisation and strengthening of the organisation

Montani AS
Fridtjof Nansens Plass 4
N-0160 Oslo
Norway
Tel: +47 2282 8660
Fax: +47 2282 8661

Graham Wason is an independent travel and tourism adviser specialising in the Nordic countries.

Egholmen 11
3400 Hillerod
Denmark
Tel and Fax: +45 4824 2688

Cossington Park
Bridgwater
Somerset TA7 8LH
UK
Tel and Fax: +44 (0)1278 723474

Mark Woods works at the Trade Development Centre, the export development agency for central Scotland.

Mark Woods
Trade Development Centre
Willow House
Newhouse Road
Grangemouth
FK3 8LL
UK
Tel: +44 (0)1324 499500
Fax: +44 (0)1324 499501
E-mail: tdc@scotexport.org.uk
Website http://scotexport.org.uk/

Foreword

This book is timely; there has probably never been a better time to sell to Scandinavia and the Nordic countries. Yet many British companies have overlooked this market on their doorstep. The message is now getting through; Scandinavia is an ideal market, both for experienced exporters and also smaller companies who may be selling abroad for the first time.

With a population of over 23 million and amongst the highest per capita GDP in the world it offers a tempting market. The Nordic economies have recovered from the recessions of the early '90s and are now growing fast. Business is booming, and there are good opportunities for UK exporters in just about every sector. The economy shows no signs of slowing yet, nor overheating; inflation is low.

What benefits do British exporters enjoy here? English is widely spoken, proximity (Scandinavia is closer to NE England and Scotland than anywhere else on the continent), very similar business practices, and a receptive market with a wide knowledge of all things British through our media, sport and culture among other things. Access could not be easier.

This book examines in more detail why the Scandinavian market is so attractive for British companies, and highlights some of the sectors and opportunities of particular interest. I hope it will convince existing exporters here that they are doing the right thing, and persuade new ones that it is high time they investigated this market on their doorstep. I am sure that you will be very pleasantly surprised.

As in any market, you are more likely to succeed if you prepare yourself before coming. The DTI and our Embassies' Commercial Sections are there to help, and will be happy to offer UK firms advice, market research and a wide range of practical assistance designed to help you to enter the market and, we hope, do good business here.

Anne Woodward
Deputy Director for the Benelux, Republic of Ireland and the Nordic region, Department of Trade and Industry.

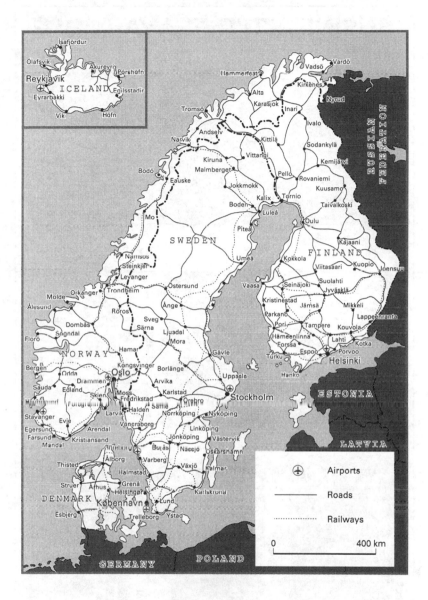

Map of Scandinavia

BUSINESS TITLES AVAILABLE

Part 1

Outlook for Exporters

Nordic Cash Management:
One Bank, One System, One Second

Den Danske Bank's Nordic Cash Management philosophy is as unique as it is simple: Four countries, one bank, one system in one second.

Our office banking system, DanskeBank TeleService, enables you to make payments directly from Great Britain between the four Nordic countries as though there were no borders.

When using DanskeBank TeleService you are on-line with the Bank's central IT-systems. Direct communication with Den Danske Bank's systems enables you to economise on your administration and on your costs while you benefit from more interest days.

Please contact us for more information on how to optimise your Nordic Cash Management with DanskeBank TeleService.

DEN DANSKE BANK

London Branch
75 King William Street
London EC4N 7DT
Tel. 0171 410 8093

1

Market Potential

Ole H. Christensen, Commercial Officer,
British Embassy, Copenhagen

Why export?

Your first question really should be, 'Why export?' And indeed why should you? If your home market still offers as much opportunity as your firm can cope with, you may be wiser to cover that demand first. Exporting does, of course, spread the risk. Declining demand in one market may be replaced by increasing demand in another. And once you are established in export markets, you will be meeting overseas competition on its own ground, and will have more confidence that your home market is not suddenly going to be undermined by imports.

The decision to commence exporting is neither easy nor one which should be taken lightly. The export market has to be seen as an extension of your natural market, not one you can sell to when the home market is a little slow and then forget about when it picks up again. You must, from the start, be as committed to the export market as you are to the home market. Remember that if there is a demand it will be satisfied. If you do not satisfy it, your competitors will be there, ready and more than willing.

Professional exporters are successful because they plan their entry into new markets. They research and choose the markets carefully and then give them their full commitment. If you enter, leave and then re-enter a market your commitment to it will be questioned. Make sure you can stay and support it. A British ice-cream maker started investigating Scandinavia a few years ago and then found that a hot British summer meant that he did not have the capacity to service his new market. Make sure that you are not caught out by this sort of problem.

Do not be one of the 'creamers' who try to pick up a bit of export sales here and there in an untargeted and unfocused manner when you can fit it in. This is counterproductive and the effort expended often does not justify the profits made. You have to make the commitment.

If you are going to export, why choose the Nordic region? It has an affluent, well-educated population with a liking for well-designed, imaginative quality products. All the countries in the region are advanced industrial economies, but small ones. This means that they will not have a complete industrial base and will always depend on imports for some supplies and components. For instance, there are no manufacturers of active electronic components in Denmark. It is also an area strong in high-tech manufacture and R&D companies and institutions with whom British R&D enterprises can form rewarding alliances.

English is widely spoken and invoices are paid very promptly. However, it is not good enough just to rely on being British – although the British image can work well with names like Burberry, Barbour and Mulberry.

Primarily Scandinavians will buy on:

- quality;
- price;
- design;
- ability to deliver on time.

It is vital that exporters do not do someone a favour and squeeze in an extra job, which then makes everybody else's late. Scandinavian customers will be very unforgiving if delivery dates are missed. German and Swedish companies are very good at working to just-in-time delivery programmes and British companies must match them.

How big is the potential market?

But how big is the new export market? By using the formula *local production + imports – exports = total market supply* you can begin to visualise the size of your market. By having figures for the last three years you can see how your market has developed. Now you can imagine a trend for the future and can make up your own mind by asking, 'Do I want a piece of the action here?' Do not equivocate – remember that if there is a demand, there is also somebody satisfying it, somewhere. You need to research who that somebody is and the DTI and your local British Embassy can help. There are a number of cost-effective services that we offer:

1. *For £100 your embassy abroad will perform up to four hours of research.* This is the typical cost for a 'cold' list of potential distributors and agents.
2. *For £200 your embassy abroad will perform up to eight hours of research.* That will buy you 2 'cold' lists.
3. *For £300 your embassy abroad will perform up to twelve hours of research.* That gives the necessary time to do a detailed and thorough job for you.
4. *For £600 your embassy abroad will perform up to 24 hours of research.* This gives us even more time to do a detailed and meticulous job which will include: competitor details, potential agents and distributors with status reports and unsuitable ones eliminated, relevant standards, rules and regulations.
5. *For £1,200 your embassy abroad will perform over 48 hours of research, and each additional 24 hours' work costs £600.* It is rare that research in a small country such as Denmark requires that length of time.

Options 3 and 4 are probably the most cost effective. Full details of these services are given in Chapter 11, 'Sources of Information'.

Market potential

You will also have to decide on the market potential for your product or service. The British Overseas Trade Board (BOTB), part of the government's Overseas Trade Services, has produced a list of priority areas for each country (see Table 1.1) and this is probably

Table 1.1 *BOTB priority areas*

	Denmark	Finland	Iceland	Norway	Sweden
Automotive components and accessories	✓		✓		
Civil engineering:					
Airport development	✓			✓	
Aluminium smelter extension			✓		
Building materials			✓	✓	✓
Components		✓			✓
Construction	✓				✓
Tunnel project			✓		
Clothing:	✓	✓	✓	✓	✓
Mail order clothing					✓
Computer software	✓				
Education and training					✓
Electronic components	✓	✓			
Energy		✓			
Environment:				✓	
Equipment and technology	✓				
Waste management	✓				
Water and wastewater			✓		✓
Financial services		✓			✓
Food and drink:	✓	✓	✓	✓	✓
Organic food	✓				
Gardening equipment	✓				
Giftware	✓				
Houseware – mail order		✓			✓
Interior fittings		✓			
Medical – equipment for disabled	✓		✓	✓	
Paper					✓
Printing					✓
Public procurement					✓
Security		✓			✓
Sport and leisure		✓			
Telecommunications	✓		✓	✓	✓
Transport:					
Railways and equipment	✓			✓	
Shipbuilding components	✓	✓			

a good place to start. However, to find out more about the threats and opportunities it is always best to talk to someone on the ground and here again the commercial officers at your embassy abroad can help.

So exporting to the Nordic region offers real opportunities. It is a demanding market with high standards but a dedicated exporter with the right product will reap handsome rewards. And if you can sell your product in Scandinavia, it has met a quality standard that means it will sell worldwide.

2

Areas of Opportunity

Mark Woods, Trade Development Centre
(with additional material from Reino Routamo,
Interdevelopment Oy and the DTI)

Denmark

Population: 5.2 million
GDP: US$162 billion
Language: Danish
Time: GMT +1
Euro Zone: No

Denmark is a small country with a sophisticated industrial economy. It has managed to avoid the recession experienced elsewhere in Europe, mainly by achieving high levels of industrial exports. In recent years, growth has been approximately 2.5 per cent a year. Since 1990 Denmark has maintained a substantial balance of payments. Politically stable, Denmark's coalition government has reduced unemployment while maintaining an advanced health and social security system as a priority. It hopes to achieve these aims through reform of economic, taxation and labour market policy, education and training.

UK trade with Denmark is now in balance after many years of deficit. Ease of access and communication (English is widely spoken), together with a strong cultural and historic affinity, make

Denmark an ideal market for British companies, not least for SMEs with no previous exporting experience.

Incentives for market entry

Improved infrastructure links across Denmark and to neighbouring countries will increase its significance as a hub for other Scandinavian markets and the Baltic States.

Most important natural resources

Denmark's most important natural resources are petroleum, natural gas, fish, molybdenum, cryolite and agriculture.

Export opportunities

Danes feel very close to the UK and, broadly speaking, any product that sells well in the UK will sell in Denmark. Areas of particular potential include machinery and equipment, chemical products, vehicles, automotive components and accessories, plastics, aircraft and parts, marine equipment and shipbuilding components, packaging and processing machinery, fuels, coal, industrial chemicals, electronic and metal industries and theme park equipment.

High-tech products
Areas of potential here include computer hardware, peripherals, software and services, telecommunications equipment, electronic components, process controls, oil and gasfield machinery, electronic production and test equipment, advanced medical and laboratory equipment.

Consumer goods
Important here will be food and drink (including alcohol), seafood, tools and DIY equipment, gardening, giftware and clothing.

Projects
Opportunities will exist in oil field refurbishment and directional drilling.

Most promising investment opportunities
Of particular relevance here are information technology, transport and construction projects and the food industries.

Finland

Population: 5 million
GDP: US$118 billion
Languages: Finnish, Swedish
Time: GMT +2
Euro Zone: Yes

Finland enjoys a high standard of living, comparable to the rest of the Nordic region, and is recovering from the recession of the early 1990s, which was severe and followed a long period of continuous growth in its economy. Strong export performance has led this recovery, focusing on both traditional and technology exports. The mainstay of the Finnish economy continues to be the timber industry and its secondary spin-offs. These include the paper and pulp industry, process engineering and energy. The vast majority of businesses (99.5 per cent) are SMEs employing fewer than 200 people, and a privatisation programme of larger industries has been drawn up. Public sector agencies and business generally prefer to deal with local agents/importers, although direct import is most common. English is widely spoken in business circles, and trade has increased in both directions between the UK and Finland. Paper and oil sales represent a large proportion of this trade.

Incentives for market entry

EU membership has further eroded protection and restrictive legislation in the Finnish economy, though some products (textiles in particular) are still restricted to non-EU countries. Investment is now actively encouraged and priority sectors have been identified in telecommunications, food, components, textiles and inward investment. Capital investment is growing at an annual rate of 25 per cent and consumer expenditure at over 4 per cent. Finland's industrial base is becoming more characterised by world-class technological innovation which provides promising ground for joint

ventures and technology transfer. There is 'gateway' trade with
Russia and Baltic States, especially Estonia, with which there are
cultural and ethnic links.

Most important natural resources

The most important natural resources in Finland are wood, peat,
copper, zinc, iron ore, vanadium and hydroelectric power.

Export opportunities

Opportunities exist in the fields of aircraft and parts, shipbuilding
components, raw materials, fuels, chemicals including industrial,
electronic components, electronic and metal industries, machinery,
vehicles and engineering supplies to powerful export industries.

High-tech products
Areas of potential include computer hardware, peripherals, software
and services, telecommunications equipment, electronic components, process controls, oil and gasfield machinery, electronic
production and test equipment, advanced medical and laboratory
equipment.

Consumer goods
Important here are food and drink (including alcohol), seafood,
clothing, interior fittings and tools and DIY equipment.

Services
Opportunities exist in the financial and consultancy and design
services.

Most promising investment opportunities
Relevant here are biotechnology and other high-tech industries,
printing, logistics, quality consumer goods, healthcare and healthcare industries, Arctic technologies and construction.

Harold Formstone, Commercial Officer at the British Embassy in
Helsinki adds:
A large part of Finnish trade was always with the Soviet Union –
the collapse of this trade between 1990 and 1992 was one of the

causes of the severe recession in Finland in 1991–1993, when output fell by 12 per cent. Finland has since made a strong recovery, and, having joined the EU in 1995, is much more orientated towards western Europe. The economy is now strong and growing at around 3.4 per cent a year. The only major problem is a relatively high level of unemployment, although this is falling. Finland joined the ERM in October 1996 and is a founder member of the new Euro Zone. Indeed, with Luxembourg, it is the only country that entered without a major fudge of the Maastricht criteria.

A strong balance of payments surplus and increasing consumer confidence linked with low inflation means that the Finnish market is in good shape, both as regards capital investment and consumer demand. In 1997 order books moved strongly above the trend line showing an improvement of more than 10 per cent over normal levels, being particularly strong in forest (paper and timber), basic metals, electronics and the electrical industries. Investment expectations are mixed and although up overall there are differences between sectors: basic metal expects a significant rise while paper, wood products, chemical and construction expect to decrease. Capacity utilisation is running at a fraction under 90 per cent.

Production and ex-factory prices are very stable although there might be small increase in 1998. Given the strength of the pound this could cause competitive problems for UK exporters. With its high-tech industries, but comparatively small industrial base, Finland is a good area for industrial co-operation, either in manufacturing, R&D or service provision.

Iceland

Population: 270,000
GDP: US$7.3 billion
Language: Icelandic
Time: GMT (no daylight saving in the summer)
Euro Zone: No

Although the country has a population of only 270,000, there is a high per capita income among its sophisticated consumers, who have a demonstrable taste for innovative, high-quality products and services. The country is politically stable and heavily dependent on imported consumer goods and industrial equipment. The economy has historically been natural resources led, with fish accounting for 75 per cent of 1997 exports. Metals are becoming increasingly important to Iceland's production economy, with resulting opportunities in supplying equipment and chemical products.

Incentives for market entry

Iceland is a welcoming venue for the first-time exporter, being a compact market with an almost universal knowledge of English. The market is heavily dependent on imports, and the signing of the EEA agreement has resulted in liberalisation and improved opportunities in a number of sectors. There are no longer restrictions on foreign investment and capital movement, but there remain some restrictions on inward investment in the fishing industry.

There are heavy tariffs on primary food products and the import of meat and dairy products is banned. However, there are opportunities in processed food.

Export opportunities

The Icelandic market is very close in taste to the UK and products that sell well in Britain will sell well in Iceland. Areas of particular potential include food-processing machinery, electrical machinery, marine engines, fishing tackle, shipboard electronics, oil, health-care and management training.

High-tech products
Of potential here are personal computers and software, telecommunications, telephones (including cellular), medical equipment, engines and tractors and automotive components.

Consumer goods
Important here are consumer electronics, processed food and drink, clothing (including children's and leisurewear), hand tools and other high-quality consumer goods.

Projects
There are also opportunities in sewage treatment and airport, power and road tunnel projects.

Tom Burnham, the DTI Export Promoter for the Nordic countries adds:
Iceland is a relatively easy market for British companies to enter. English is widely spoken, Icelanders are very friendly and the British are popular – furthermore our main competitors, Norway and Germany, are less visible than the UK. Iceland has a population of 270,000, but with high spending habits it is more like 600,000. The UK is also the major overseas shopping destination with 30,000 visiting Glasgow – the nearest international airport – and 60,000 visiting London every year. Icelanders are predisposed to buy British goods. There is also very little indigenous competition. If the British Embassy confirms that a market exists for your product you should be able to secure an order for at least £10,000. Like all Nordic countries they pay on time.

The country should not really have been called Iceland as its climate is very similar to Scotland.

There are opportunities in both goods and services. The Icelanders are great experts in water management and this is probably the one area where there are no opportunities. Management training is another very fruitful area.

Norway

Population: 4.3 million
GDP: US$153 billion
Language: Norwegian
Time: GMT +1
Euro Zone: No

Norway enjoys one of the highest standards of living in Europe, thanks mainly to natural resources offshore and hydropower on the mainland. The importance of the country's energy reserves and its secondary industry cannot be understated, but there is large investment in developing new areas of commerce, to guard against oil price fluctuation. A decline in traditional manufacturing industry has been countered by a rise in service industries, which now account for 30 per cent of GDP, and advanced technology industries are also growing.

The structure of Norway's international trade reflects the importance of oil and gas to its own economy. Paper and wood products, chemicals and metal products are also significant, and machinery manufacture is the single most important area. Consumers are price sensitive, and discounting has been successful.

Incentives for market entry

The fact that Norway has remained outside the EU brings with it both pros and cons. Free trade continues to exist due to the European Economic Area accords, and there is an open attitude to foreign products. However, quotas and tariffs do exist in some areas. Safety and environmental standards are strict, and tastes in consumer goods can vary a great deal from British ones. Exporters may have to accept initial low profit margins, and invest time in research and marketing to succeed in the long term.

There are very high tariff barriers that prevent the import of primary foodstuffs. Norwegians will normally only buy high-value capital goods or projects through joint ventures where one partner is Norwegian.

Extensive Norwegian statistics are available at http://www.ssb. no/www-open/english/yearbook/

Export opportunities

Opportunities exist in the fields of high-tech machinery and equipment, aircraft, industrial raw materials, oil and gas technology and offshore petroleum development equipment, communications equipment and pharmaceuticals.

Consumer goods
Of importance here are high-quality consumer goods, food and fruit and vegetables.

Sweden

Population: 8.7 million
GDP: US$270 billion
Language: Swedish
Time: GMT +1
Euro Zone: No

In the post-war period Sweden was renowned for achieving the unique combination of economic growth, high standards of living and social welfare protection. In the late 1980s, however, Swedish industry fared poorly, especially in the service sectors. This was followed by a severe recession, which forced a change in economic policy, notably with programmes of investment in high technology and R&D.

The main sectors of production include metals, textiles, chemicals, paper and pulp, electronics, telecommunications and motor vehicles.

Incentives for market entry

The Swedish public procurement market is significant with a value of £22 billion per annum (see Chapter 10). British industrial goods can be imported without a licence, but most agricultural and chemical goods do require one. English is widely spoken. Products are expected to be of high quality and to respect environmental standards.

Most important natural resources

Sweden's most important natural resources are iron ore, zinc, hydroelectric power, lead, wood, silver and fish.

Export opportunities

Opportunities exist in machinery, vehicles, aircraft and parts, defence industry equipment, medical equipment and supplies, mechanical, industrial and electronic engineering, engineering components, textiles, tourism, agricultural products and chemicals.

High-tech products
Computers, peripherals, and software telecommunications services are important here.

Consumer goods
Food and drink, tobacco, clothing, footwear and other high-quality consumer goods offer potential.

Public procurement
Especially relevant here are the security and health sectors.

Services
Services such as design and financial consultancy, water treatment and infrastructure projects are important.

Most promising investment opportunities
Opportunities abound in healthcare, automotive, forestry and wood products, steel, IT and telecommunications.

Thanks are due to Harold Formstone, Commercial Officer at the British Embassy in Helsinki, and Tom Burnham, DTI Export Promoter for Iceland, Denmark and Norway, for their contributions to this chapter.

3

Iceland: Cool Trade Opportunities

Stefan S. Gudjonsson, Secretary General of the Federation of Icelandic Trade

History and marketing

One of history's boldest marketing ploys was implemented by the Icelandic Viking, Eric the Red. Intent upon colonising the vast, ice-covered land he had discovered west of Iceland, he decided to name it Greenland in hopes of attracting more settlers. The settlers soon realised what most people know today: in spite of its name, Iceland is covered in green, while Greenland is covered in ice. With the warm waters of the Gulf Stream flowing around it, Iceland's average winter temperature is comparable to New York or Boston. So do not be put off doing business with Iceland because of the weather and the name.

And, to continue in the same vein, do not be put off doing business with Iceland because of the size of its market. With one of the highest per capita incomes in the world and with nearly half of the population concentrated in or around the capital city, Reykjavik, Icelanders enjoy some of the strongest buying power in Europe. Iceland has a highly developed consumer market in a well-organised western society, with forward-thinking businesses and along democratic tradition. Culturally speaking, Icelanders are Nordic and have had strong associations with the other Scandinavian countries. Anglo–American influences can also be found.

The economy and trade

The Icelandic economy is currently booming: in 1997 the economy grew by 5 per cent and the forecast for 1998 is a further 4.6 per cent increase. Due in part to a significant increase in long-term foreign investment in the power industries, there is every reason to believe that this trend will continue for some time. It is, therefore, an ideal time to start doing business with Iceland and we encourage all UK companies to take Iceland into serious consideration. One important area where British retailers are doing well is in franchising (see Chapter 19). As Icelanders are keen travellers, they are much acquainted with British retail stores. On the whole, Britain is an important trading partner of Iceland and has been so all this century.

Currently, foreign trade accounts for nearly 70 per cent of GNP which is very high by international standards. This is due to the fact that Iceland exports most of its produce and needs to import more or less all necessities, consumer goods and investment goods alike. The export of fish is still very important, accounting for nearly 70 per cent of the total export value, but new important export products include aluminium, ferro-alloy and specialised high-tech equipment and software for the fishing/food industry. Iceland is also an important producer of cheap geothermal and hydroelectric power with vast energy resources which to date have been only partially utilised.

Iceland imports a wide variety of consumer products such as food and beverages, textiles, building materials, giftware, medical supplies, furniture, cosmetics, and investment goods such as computers, machinery, fishing gear, electric supplies and raw materials. These products are normally imported through agents who frequently also act as distributors. This is possible due to the relative ease of distribution in Iceland once products are in the country. The importer/agent normally represents several brands or manufacturers, but rarely competing brands. This is necessary in order to create viable business volumes. In some areas of trade, retailers may be importing directly as in speciality sectors such as clothing and giftware, where a product may only be sold in one or two stores and not through mass distribution.

Iceland is not a member of the EU but joined the European Economic Area (EEA) in 1994 together with the other European Free Trade Association (EFTA) countries. As a result, there are no tariffs on imported manufactured goods from Europe to Iceland. Basic VAT rate is 24.5 per cent with an elaborate system of excise duties on selected products. Iceland also has a well-established and reliable banking system. Payment terms in international trade can be anything from open account to bank draft or letter of credit. Credit information can be obtained from credit agencies such as Dunn and Bradstreet.

As you can see, Iceland is a growing and vital economy with tremendous development potential. My office at the Federation of Icelandic Trade welcomes all enquiries and we are pleased to help you find a suitable business partner in Iceland.

4

Export Winners

A number of small and medium-sized British companies have entered the Scandinavian market in the last few years. They have all found it a good market to do business in. The Scandinavians are friendly and straightforward people – however, they are not pushovers when it come to negotiating. As the following exporters discovered, a good product that is marketed and promoted properly will be a success.

Case Study 1
Beverage Brands (UK) Ltd

Beverage Brands (UK) Ltd is the British-based manufacturer of alcoholic and non-alcoholic drinks. They are best known for *Caledonian Clear*, a sparkling flavoured spring water, *Rudees*, a fruit soda, and *Woodys* and *WKD*, alcoholic carborates. The company has been successfully exporting their range to Scandinavian countries for several years where they have distributors in all countries.

In 1994, Finland was the only Scandinavian market for *Caledonian Clear* but in 1995 a successful Trade Mission to Stockholm introduced the company to an up-and-coming American food importer who was looking for successful water-based products to add to their growing portfolio. Today, Sweden is one of the company's major importers of *Caledonian Clear*, and *Rudees*. Beverage Brands has established successful distributors in Finland and Iceland. Finding a distributor for the alcoholic drinks range in Sweden and Norway is now a priority for the company.

Apart from trade shows and missions, Beverage Brands is using a much more proactive approach to finding new distributors. After initial country research, specific companies are evaluated and targeted on the basis of financial information, existing complementary product range and distribution channels. Beverage Brands has a corporate CD-ROM which it targets at prospective distributors and also sends specific presentations and samples to short-listed companies.

Scandinavia has proved to be one of the most successful regions of Western Europe for the company's products. However, issues such as national labelling restrictions, language requirements and local bottling regulations need to be considered by the first-time exporter, despite most Scandinavian countries being European Union members. In addition, many countries have their own idiosyncrasies that need to be addressed, such as different drinking ages (Iceland).

To handle the increase in export business and to increase personal contact, Beverage Brands appointed an International Sales Manager in 1997 and looks forward to introducing their new products *Woodys World of Cocktails* and *WKD Slam* to Scandinavian customers soon.

Case Study 2
Selectamark

Jim Brown is the MD of Selectamark Security Systems of Locksbottom, Kent. Although Selectamark had been selling its permanent, visual property marking equipment into the Scandinavian market for over a decade it had not entered the Finnish market. When Finland joined the EU Selectamark took part in a Public Security Equipment and Services Exhibition organised by the DTI and the Home Office in Helsinki and Stockholm in May 1997. This enabled Selectamark to identify a Finnish distributor and its system is now being used in hospitals, schools and government departments.

Selectamark has always used distributors to enter a new market as it is then able to use someone who is aware of local market conditions and who will normally finance its own operation. A distributor needs good product know-how to succeed. Today Selectamark has 29 distributors around the world and in some markets, such as Australia, fully owned subsidiaries have been created to manage the distributors.

Selectamark has found that distributors in Scandinavia are very trustworthy and loyal to the product. They can also be aggressive in their
market plan. In Denmark, there are 32 competitors, many of whom are
local, but the distributor has ensured that Selectamark remains the market
leader in its field.

The products comply with international and EU regulations such as CHIP I
and 2, although the ISO9000 series is often seen as the most important,
especially when introducing new products into new markets.

5

Lessons of Market Entry

Basic principles

There are some basic principles in entering a new market:

- Do your research. Does your product fit the market? If not, why not? Can it be tailored to the market?
- Your export promoter, the DTI Nordic Desk and the local British embassy will all help you explore the local market. There are also many local sources of information (see Chapter 11).
- Visit your prospective market. There are many trade visits and shows that you can use (see Chapter 12).
- Use the visit to see as many potential customers as possible.
- Identify a local agent or distributor (see Chapter 17).
- Manage the agents or distributors. If you do not show any interest in them, they will not show any in your product.
- Make sure that you can serve the market. Will you be able to cope with unexpected demand on your home market? It is more difficult to re-enter a market if you are seen not to have commitment to it because of a past failure.
- Consider using the Internet as a sales, promotion and support mechanism.

Case Study I

A UK exporter called at the British Embassy in Copenhagen having just left a meeting with the company's Danish distributor and found out why it had sold nothing in the three years since the contract had been signed. The distributor had 80 employees and 111 agencies (i.e. 1.4 agencies per employee). Worse still they were distributors for the UK exporter's major competitor. If he had done his homework, or contacted the Embassy, he could have been forewarned of the danger of using that distributor.

Case Study 2
Epigem Ltd

Dr Tim Ryan is MD of Epigem, a small two-year-old specialist opto-electronics company based in Middlesbrough. Together with four other SMEs he went on an electronics sector visit, organised by Rob Allaker of the County Durham Development Company (see Chapter 11), to Finland in January 1998 where they also attended the 'Electrometal' Interprise event in Turku.

Epigem is looking for sales to companies such as Nokia as well as R&D co-operation with Finnish companies that could then lead to joint export drives into other markets. It already had some Nordic contacts made in the European Eureka programme and this visit was an opportunity to visit one in its home base and to visit an exhibition containing samples of official products supplied to a Finnish designer.

Tim Ryan also wanted to understand how the Nokia supply chain worked. Nokia described this at the Interprise event. He has found in the past that for his sort of company initial contacts with potential large customers are often made through the research arm. But whatever the initial approach, it is essential that you understand the potential customer and how it works before you start your approach.

All the attendees at Interprise, both Finnish and foreign, were essentially small fish seeking to feed off the bigger fish in the pond. Tim and his Finnish partner are considering forming a European economic interest group (EEIG) to design and manufacture optical components. This is a special form of transnational partnership that allows companies from different European nations to co-operate and work together.

Epigem uses its web site (http://ourworld.compuserve.com/homepages/ epigem) to promote its technical expertise. This has led to a number of fruitful enquiries from the USA, Germany and Switzerland.

Case Study 3
Pride Valley Foods Limited

Pride Valley Foods is a producer of Indian naan breads, Pitta breads, and Mexican Flour Tortillas. It already exports to a limited degree mainly into Belgium and Germany, and in seeking to identify the next market for speciality breads they selected the Nordic region. Through the Northern Food and Drinks Federation and the Northern Development Company, Pride Valley was put in touch with Tom Burnham (00 +44 (0)1835 830 758), an export promoter at the DTI. As part of a tour of the North East he visited and suggested Iceland as a market. In conjunction with Orn Valdimarsson of the British Embassy they contacted the Marketing Manager of an Icelandic bakery who had expressed interest when Pride Valley exhibited their product range at the I.F.E. some months earlier in London. This support prompted the bakery to research their market potential with consumer focus groups. Following encouraging results the Iceland team and Pride Valley moved very quickly to design artwork, and proceed to launch three products within the market.

In general the identification of new markets is based on looking at areas where an awareness of Indian and Mexican foods is growing, and the market is of a size that the company can sensibly tackle – both as regards the ability to produce the product to meet demand and being small enough to manage easily. Orn Valdimarsson of the British Embassy in Reykjavik makes the point that Iceland is a good test market, as not only is it reasonably small; it also has the fifth highest spending per capita in the world.

Pride Valley was able to supply its standard UK product with a label change.

Part 2

Sector Prospects

6

Industrial Sales

Denmark

Danish business life is dominated by small and medium sized companies and over 75 per cent of Danish industrial companies employ fewer than 50 people. This is considered an advantage because the lines of communication are short, which can simplify the selling process for would-be suppliers to Danish industry. The larger European market is starting to encourage mergers and there is evidence of Danish companies forming alliances, which enable them to increase their size in the market without losing their independence.

In 1972 Denmark was the first country to create a Ministry for the Environment and it still has the highest per capita spending on pollution and environmental control. The EU Environment Agency is situated in Copenhagen and the Danes are world leaders in this field. There will be opportunities for joint ventures and the supply of specialist components.

A privatisation programme is underway with a number of state-owned assets being sold either partially or in full. These include Tele Danmark and Copenhagen Airport. Additionally, some state enterprises, such as the loss-making railways, are being converted into profit centres.

Historically, Denmark spends less than the EU average on R&D, but has always been ready to import R&D. Investment in machinery and equipment in 1996 was approximately $11.5 billion. Denmark has an ageing oilfield where there is a need for replacement parts and refurbishment equipment. The UK, along with Germany and the USA, is a major supplier. There will also be a need for directional drilling equipment to extract the remaining reserves.

The need to cut costs in Denmark's highly efficient medical services should offer opportunities for labour-saving equipment. In general there is a demand for high-tech diagnostic and surgical equipment.

Active industrial sectors include:

● biotechnology;
● energy conservation;
● environmental protection including wastewater purification systems;
● incineration plants;
● wind turbine technology.

Other prospects for goods and services include:

● information technology;
● electrical power systems. Danish standards are very high, but they are also very dependent on imports of oil and gasfield machinery (for refurbishment of existing field);
● medical equipment;
● telecommunications equipment.

Finland

Rapid export growth has prompted expansion of manufacturing capacity in recent years. Machinery and equipment investment increased by a further 5 per cent in 1997. Machinery equipment investment activity will decrease as the expansion of capacity in the paper and basic metal industries is completed. As well as its basic industries, especially forestry products, Finland has a large high-tech sector, but a comparatively small industrial base.

In the last quarter of 1997 investments in machinery and equipment grew by 13.5 per cent, and in construction by nearly 15 per cent compared to the corresponding period in 1996.

Production and ex-factory prices are very stable although there might be a small increase in 1998. Given the strength of the pound this could cause competitive problems for UK exporters. With its high-tech industries but comparatively small industrial base Finland is a good area for industrial co-operation, in either manufacturing, R&D or service provision.

Sales opportunities

Food processing now constitutes the third largest industrial sector. With nine countries in reach by road transport within 24 hours the industry has established a sizeable presence in nearby markets.

Other sales opportunities include:

- hi-tech industry;
- electronics, including components;
- telecommunications;
- information technology;
- medical technology;
- natural resources-related industry;
- environment;
- healthcare;
- castings, forgings, pumps and valves.

Joint ventures

Investors are increasingly looking in Finland's booming technology industries for partners with whom they can collaborate. This applies to both R&D and joint sales partnerships. Science parks around the universities have increased the number of spin-off companies carrying out R&D. Some lack venture capital and a market-orientated business approach and need help to reach overseas markets.

Finnish companies cover a wide range, including:

- computers and office equipment;
- software development;
- telecommunications (Finland has the world's only entirely digital telecommunications network);
- control and instrumentation;
- medical electronics;
- components and sub-assemblies;
- cables and wires;
- fixtures;

- power technology;
- consumer electronics;
- lighting equipment and devices.

Output

Total output increased by 4.1 per cent in the year to January 1998. The *Monthly Indicator of Total Output* (of *Statistics Finland*) shows that output went up in all main branches of industry, with the exception of agriculture and forestry. There was an almost 10 per cent rise in output in the manufacturing industry.

Growth (the fourth quarter of 1997 compared to the quarter of 1996):

- wood and paper industry grew by over 13 per cent;
- metal industry by 14.5 per cent;
- primary production increased by over 9.5 per cent;
- construction grew by 11.5 per cent;
- transport by over 8 per cent.

The growth of exports moderated towards the end of the year, falling to just below 9 per cent in the final quarter of 1997. The growth of imports also slowed down from the previous year, to stand at just short of 8 per cent.

Iceland

Iceland has a comparatively small manufacturing sector at 11 per cent of GDP, as opposed to a more normal 20 per cent. The country imports a wide variety of investment goods, normally through agents who frequently also act as distributors. This is possible due to the relative ease of distribution in Iceland once products are in the country. The importer/agent normally represents several brands or manufacturers, but rarely competing brands. This is necessary in order to create viable business volumes.

The small manufacturing sector is balanced by a very large fishing sector and there are opportunities to supply this.

Iceland is energy rich with both geothermal and hydroelectric supplies. This has led to energy-dependent industries such as aluminium smelting at Hrauneyjarfoss. There is potential to supply these industries.

Major import sectors include:

- textiles and yarn (dominated by German imports);
- building materials;
- food-processing machinery;
- electrical machinery;
- marine engines;
- fishing tackle;
- shipboard electronics;
- medical equipment;
- medical supplies;
- healthcare;
- scientific equipment;
- management training;
- transport equipment (dominated by German imports);
- engines and tractors;
- automotive components;
- chemicals;
- mineral fuels and lubricants;
- paper (dominated by Swedish and German imports);
- iron and steel (dominated by Swedish and German imports);
- non-ferrous metals.

Norway

Norway's industry is dominated by oil (20 per cent of GDP), fishing and shipping, together with an important public sector. It is western Europe's largest producer of fish and oil. With new oilfields coming on stream in 1998 investment in oil and shipping rose by about 40 per cent in mid-1997, although this dropped to about 18 per cent towards the end of the year. Oil exploration is set to continue in 1998. Real GDP continues to grow at a rapid rate – 4.8 per cent in 1996, 3.6 per cent in 1997 and 3.3 per cent in 1998 (estimate).

Activity in the house building sector is buoyant, with a consequent demand for building materials and fittings.

There is a tight labour market, with a consequent pressure on wages. There are also a number of labour disputes, especially in the oil and gas industry.

Because of the dominance of the offshore sector, there is an imbalance in Norwegian industry. Many sectors that do not support the oil and gas industry are under-represented and these areas should offer opportunities for industrial exports. Non-oil industry accounts for about 20 per cent of GDP and is strongest in chemicals, engineering and timber products.

Norwegian imports by category in 1995

- Machinery, equipment and miscellaneous manufactured goods (54 per cent);
- industrial inputs (39 per cent).

Areas of opportunity will include:

- specialised high-tech machinery;
- industrial process controls;
- other machinery and equipment;
- laboratory scientific instruments;
- medical equipment;
- data-processing and office equipment, peripherals and software;
- telecommunications equipment;
- chemicals;
- pollution control equipment (including water and sewage purification);
- oil and gas technology;
- industrial raw materials;
- airport and ground support equipment;
- aircraft and parts;
- defence equipment.

Sweden

The growth in real GDP, which is running at 2.5–3 per cent in 1997–98, is being driven in part by higher exports, with very little growth coming from the public sector where spending is being reduced to meet Maastricht criteria. Increasing domestic consumption is also helping. This has led to increased stock building in the industrial and commercial sectors.

There has been better than average to strong growth in telecommunications products, machinery, chemicals, wood products, steel and non-ferrous metal products. The increase in machinery production reflects the growth in industrial investment and capital formation.

Modern Swedish industry is increasingly dominated by high value added production. Industrial sales will need to address these areas.

Sweden will stay outside the Euro Zone, at least in the short term. The Swedish krona has been unstable during much of the 1990s, moving from weakness at the start of the decade to comparative strength. This could affect the performance of exporters and consequent demand for industrial imports. However, there has been a steady improvement in unit labour costs since 1991, which might offset the strength of the krona.

There are three major trade fair venues in Sweden, which have a combined attendance of over 2,000,000.

Stockholmsmässan
S-125 80 Stockholm
Tel: +46 8 749 41 00
Fax: +46 8 99 20 44

Sollentunamässan
PO Box 174191 23 Sollentuna
Tel: +46 8 92 59 00
Fax: +46 8 92 97 74

The Swedish Exhibition and Congress Centre
PO Box 5222402 24 Goteborg
Tel: +46 31 708 80 00
Fax: +46 31 16 03 30

Important sectors include electronic components, especially to the telecommunications industry, telecommunication services and equipment (the Swedish telecommunications market is completely deregulated and mature), computers, peripherals and software (home ownership is starting to catch up with business use. The market is highly sophisticated and most business PCs are networked), drugs and pharmaceuticals (the local market is highly competitive and is dominated by local producers Astra and Pharmacia & Upjohn), medical equipment (with an ageing population and tighter government budgets there is a need to cut costs in this sector), analytical and scientific instruments, pollution control (Sweden's major environmental concerns are acid rain, ozone depletion and sea pollution defence equipment), motor and aircraft manufacture, aircraft and parts (Saab is the only local manufacturer, but there are opportunities to supply airlines such as SAS), and finally, clothing production has shown strong growth.

Information for this chapter has been gathered from a number of sources including the DTI, British embassies, export promoters, national statistical sources and chambers of trade.

7

Consumer Demand

Scandinavia is the home of good design and concern for the environment. As a consequence all Scandinavian and Nordic markets demand high-quality, well designed and environmentally friendly products. Technology is highly valued and almost all high-tech products will sell well.

Denmark

Consumer confidence in Denmark is mixed, having shown a sharp fall in 1996. This is mainly due to the mixed messages of falling unemployment and fluctuating inflation. However, private consumption continues to grow at about 2.5 per cent per annum.

The Danish consumer market in many ways resembles the British market and good quality products that sell well in the UK will normally sell well in Denmark, as long as the price is right.

Some Danish products are expensive by EU standards. In part this is caused by an imperfect market and lack of competition.

Of the 2.3 million households in 1994:

- 10 per cent owned a summer cottage;
- 21 per cent a telephone answering machine;
- 31 per cent a clothes drier;
- 33 per cent a personal computer;
- 35 per cent a dishwasher;
- 35 per cent a microwave oven;

- 58 per cent a compact disc player;
- 59 per cent their own house or flat;
- 67 per cent a videocassette recorder;
- 67 per cent a car (11 per cent two or more) (because of high taxes Danes tend to keep their cars for a relatively long time. This offers opportunities for car parts and service equipment);
- 73 per cent a washing machine;
- 99 per cent a telephone, television and refrigerator;
- 640,000 subscribed to a cable system for television and radio;
- 650,000 had a satellite receiver for television (1993).

Cigarette consumption declined from 7.5 billion in 1983 to 6.4 billion in 1993. During the same period, total consumption of smoking tobacco increased from 2.3 million kg to 2.9 million kg. Average consumption of pure alcohol for each Danish man, woman and child was 9.7 litres (1993). Consumption of beer, which is a national drink, and spirits is dropping but there is an increased demand for wine, consumption of which has grown from 90 million litres in 1983 to 163 million in 1997.

In 1993 11,500 books were published (Danes spend an average 45 minutes every day reading newspapers and books).

Danes spend in excess of $100 million a year on dog and cat food of which about 50 per cent is imported.

Finland

Increased economic activity in recent years has resulted in a steady rise in real disposable income and this has facilitated steady growth in consumption. Consumer expenditure is projected to rise by 3 per cent in 1997 and 1998, although tightening macroeconomic policy may reduce growth to about 2.5 per cent thereafter. Consumer sentiment in Finland is among the highest in the EU.

The rise in domestic demand is expected to sustain the trend in falling unemployment (especially in construction and private services) in the next few years and this will lead to increasing consumer demand. This will probably continue to focus on traditional areas of consumer durables, which is in the main above the EU average, and services. As in all Nordic markets high quality, well designed and environmentally friendly goods will sell well.

Opportunities include:

- high-tech areas such as:
  - electronics;
  - telecommunications;
  - PCs, peripherals and software;
- food including seafood;
- drink (including alcohol);
- clothing;
- interior fittings;
- DIY equipment and tools generally.

Iceland

Iceland's 270,000 population is among the highest consumer spending in Europe. Tom Burnham, DTI Export Promoter for Iceland, believes Icelanders have the spending power of 600,000. They have also developed a taste for UK products – they make almost 100,000 shopping trips to the UK every year.

Unemployment is low by European standards, although there is regional deviation with the rates being between 4 per cent and 1 per cent. There is evidence of sharply increased credit card purchases, although there is a parallel development of personal bank loans, presumably to finance the debt.

Iceland imports a wide variety of consumer products and, as with industrial products, they are normally imported through agents who frequently also act as distributors. This is possible due to the relative ease of distribution in Iceland once products are in the country. The importer/agent normally represents several brands or manufacturers, but rarely competing brands. This is necessary in order to create viable business volumes. In some areas of trade, retailers may be importing directly as in speciality sectors such as clothing and giftware, where a product may be sold in only one or two stores and not through mass distribution.

Taste in food is changing to a more international cuisine. There are opportunities in areas such as pasta, cereal and bread.

The Icelandic market is very close in taste to the UK and products that sell well in Britain will sell well in Iceland. Areas of particular potential include:

- computers;
- consumer electronics;
- fishing gear;
- hand tools;
- electric supplies;
- processed food and drink;
- clothing (including children's and leisurewear);
- textiles;
- giftware;
- furniture;
- cosmetics.

Norway

Thanks to higher net disposable income, which grew by 3.5 per cent in 1997, domestic consumption in Norway is on the increase. Spending by private households has increased in recent years. An increase in consumption from 1995 to 1996 occurred in all areas except for food, which is still declining and is now 13.3 per cent. People are also eating out more at restaurants.

Norwegians consumed a record amount of wine and beer in 1996. Total consumption of wine in 1996 was over 33 million litres, corresponding to 9.4 litres per capita, an increase of 7.7 per cent compared to 1995 and accounted for 22.2 per cent of total alcohol consumption. Consumption of beer increased by 3.3 per cent.

Household spending has yet to top the record set in 1987. However, the size of households is steadily decreasing and per capita consumption is higher than in 1987. Falling interest rates on home loans have reduced housing costs. Of household expenditure 22.1 per cent is spent on housing, electricity and fuel. Travel and transport, including purchases of new cars, accounts for 22.2 per cent of household expenditure. Clothing and footwear expenditure has dropped and now accounts for 6.5 per cent of household expenditure.

Opportunities include:

- food and beverages;
- manufactured consumer products;
- high-quality consumer goods.

Sweden

After five years of recession in the early 1990s, when Sweden dropped from being in the top three richest nations to nearer ten, real GDP grew by 1.3 per cent in 1996 and 2.5–3 per cent in 1997 and this rate is expected to continue in 1998. Equally, growth in domestic consumption has risen from 1.3 per cent in 1996 to approximately 2–3 per cent at the end of 1997.

Retail sales volumes are a little ahead of these figures. The growth in sales is not uniform with demand being higher in areas supplying household and DIY items. Direct selling and mail order sectors show above average growth.

After the spending spree in the 1980s personal debt rose to alarming levels. During the recession of the 1990s savings levels rose and the debt problem has been greatly reduced. However, consumers are still showing reluctance to return to their former high levels of consumption.

Sweden is a mature retail market with the percentage of domestic expenditure dedicated to basic items falling. The slowly rising consumer confidence is being reflected in an increase in purchases of more expensive discretionary items. Even in hard times consumers still demand good quality, well designed, innovative and environmentally friendly products.

Unemployment remains a problem and will continue to hold back consumer demand.

Areas of interest will include:

- food and drink;
- tobacco;
- clothing;
- sports and leisure products;
- footwear;
- other high-quality consumer goods;
- traditional British goods such as Barbour, Mulberry and Laura Ashley appeal to a traditional view of Britain that is appreciated in Sweden.

Information for this chapter has been gathered from a number of sources including the DTI, British embassies, export promoters, national statistical sources and chambers of trade.

8

Utilities and the Infrastructure in Scandinavia

Mark Johnson, SJ Berwin & Co.

The economies of the Nordic countries, Finland, Sweden, Denmark, Norway and Iceland, are expanding, with indications of major investment in industry this year. World links are being strengthened with connections with the European Union (EU), North Atlantic Treaty Organisation (NATO), the European Economic Area (EEA), and the Baltic states, all influencing development. The area contains huge strategic oil and gas reserves, which need to be exploited and developed and the Nordic triangle linking Scandinavia, Finland, St. Petersburg and Moscow is currently under construction.

Denmark

The Government has initiated large, joint venture construction projects, between Danish and foreign companies, for example, a metro system in Copenhagen and various bridges to link Denmark with Sweden and possibly Germany. European Investment Bank (EIB) loans have recently been granted to construct new bypassses and road/rail links.

Denmark is expanding into alternative energy sources, especially wind power for generating electricity. EIB loans have been granted to construct an electricity link between Denmark and Germany and to extend and modernise municipal waste treatment plants in Glostrup.

Finland

The increasing trade and economic co-operation with the EU, Russia and the Baltic states necessitates the enhancement of the country's infrastructure, especially to improve East-West rail and road links.

Early deregulation of the Finnish telecommunications markets has helped it to expand and develop quicker than most of its EU counterparts. The nation's information technology and telecommunication infrastructure (the Finnish Information Superhighway) is to be integrated into a multi-level system, incorporating schools and public services. Proposed projects are a RDS-TMC traffic information system; a GSM network for mobile multimedia applications and a satellite infrastructure within population centres.

Recent EIB loans consist of the construction of a new hydro-electric power station on the river Kitinen and the modernisation of four power stations on the river Kemijoki. The Helsinki-Tampere-Seinäjoki railway line will be upgraded, with a general emphasis on rail transport. In line with the development of the trans-European communications networks the following roads will be constructed; new sections of the E18 east-west road link and completion of the Hämeenlinna-Tampere motorway, and the upgrading to motorway standard of the E4 road link between Tornio and Kemi. A development evaluation carried out by the Finnish Road Administration stated that by 2010, 1,250 kilometres of motorway will be constructed. Only half this amount currently exists, thus invoking future investment in motorway construction.

EIB loans have also been granted for local or regional authorities for small and medium-scale infrastructure schemes in energy, transport and environmental protection.

Iceland

Iceland has extensive renewable natural resources, for example, fishing grounds and hydro-electric and geothermal power which are still exploitable. Iceland's electricity consumption per capita is one of the highest in the world, but only a fraction of the country's energy potential has been harnessed.

The EIB has recently loaned ECU 24.3 million to extend and improve wastewater collection and treatment infrastructure in Reykjavik. Previous loans have contributed towards upgrading communications and road infrastructure throughout the country.

Norway

Norway's North Sea oil and gas reserves continue to fuel growth throughout the economy as new fields are constantly discovered. For example, the recent production at Troll field will make Norway a major gas supplier to the continent for the next 50 years.

Norway's total electricity consumption is by means of hydro-electric power. Nationwide power development projects involve the construction and maintenance of reservoirs, dams, tunnel links and power lines.

An EIB loan has been granted to construct a new gasline between the Norwegian sector of the North Sea and Dunkirk in northern France. Previous loans have been granted for improving the E6 road link from Oslo to Sweden and refurbishing and extending the Ekpfisk oil and natural gas complex.

Sweden

Recent EIB loans granted to Sweden include the modernisation and expansion of the following; the electricity distribution network in Greater Stockholm and Göteborg, the drinking water supply system in Malmö, and the wastewater treatment plan in Greater Stockholm. Also funded are improvements to the sewerage, road transport and urban road infrastructure in Malmö and the modernisation of the Malmö-Göteborg west-coast railway line. Road construction involves sections of the E4 motorway between Stockholm and Helsingborg, the E6 motorway between Malmö and Svinesund and the construction of the Oresund rail/road link between Copenhagen and Malmö. Money has also been provided for the modernisation of the telecommunications network.

Sweden aims to develop a sustainable electricity production system based on renewable energy sources. Previous EIB loans funded a new combined heat and power plant fired by biofuels (mainly wood pellets), a plant for the production of wood pellets and to rehabilitate the hydropower station at Krångfors and the construction of a new hydro power station at Hednäs.

9

The Potential for UK Service Providers

Morten Tveten, Montani AS

General market description

Although a small market in global terms, the service sector in Scandinavia is well developed and in some areas quite sophisticated. e.g. computers per capita (average 227 vs UK 215), also the number of mobile telephones subscribers is well ahead of Britain (average 140 compared to 69 in UK) and the public electronic infrastructure is very well developed. From a service point of view a very rough segmentation could be:

Segments	Characteristics
IT and electronics	A very developed market, with a few large and dominant actors with global brands and many small businesses in a support role.
Personal Services	
• Tourism	Some international chains, but still very domestic with many small companies.
• Health	Public services dominant, but private sector is developing.

	Higher proportion of health professionals per capita than in UK.
● Retailing	Smaller players and not as diversified as in the UK.
Design – marketing – communication	Fairly small and less developed segment compared to the UK.
Mechanical industry	Strong professional base in Sweden, Denmark and Finland. Domestic focus.
Science and research	Strong in areas like IT and energy (3.25% of GDP in Sweden vs. 2.18% in UK), but limited to core areas.

The market is also willing to buy new services; additionally prices are mostly higher than in Britain and this offers opportunities for interesting pricing strategies. A smaller range of services and products are available in Scandinavia, which provides opportunities for UK companies who can offer better and more customer oriented concepts.

Opportunities

In the IT sector the competition is fairly tough with major US, European and Japanese actors already in place. Specialised services for key industries – like oil and gas in Norway, pulp and the specialised tool industry in Finland and Sweden and the Danish food processing industry – will in most cases welcome approaches from the UK, provided that the UK counterpart is able to come up with new and better solutions. See examples of selected opportunities below.

Segments	Opportunities
IT and electronics	A difficult market to approach unless you are a world leader with a proven record.
Personal Services ● Tourism ● Health ● Retailing	These are all areas in which personal service is all-important as this is less developed than in UK. New concepts

	especially in health and tourism are welcome. Range of services still limited versus UK, which should offer opportunities for services linked to brands and products still unknown in Scandinavia.
Design – marketing – communication	Both design – marketing – communication and mechanical industry are small and in need of
Mechanical industry	international focus and networks which could be provided by UK companies.
Science and research	A growing market. Energy, electronics and space should be of interest for UK companies.

The product and service itself is important. However in many instances Scandinavians do not always receive the personal element of service, especially in areas like the tourist industry where the individual and the understanding of personal service can be decisive. The provision of good personal service can be a key element in selling UK goods and services. Additionally, the international experience which UK companies can add will be appreciated.

Networks and approaches

As in Britain, there are both public and private organisations which are helpful and provide information free of charge. Some might even contribute aid and incentives to the British service provider. Besides the equivalent of the CBI in all countries, a good point of departure when seeking new opportunities include the following:

Organisation	Web site
SND, Norway	http://www.snd.no
NUTEK, Sweden	http://www.snd.no
ALMI, Sweden	http://www.nutek.se
KERA, Finland	http://www.kera.fi/english/hello/htm
Vaekstfonden, Denmark	http://www.vaekstfonden.dk/

All these provide financing and networking incentives

Constraints

Given the free flow of people in the EU and the EEA, there are few legal and practical constraints concerning UK companies in this sector. Note that some industry sectors may be more used to working with the British and have a better command of English. This is especially true regarding the oil and gas industry as well as tourism in all countries. The mechanical industry especially in Sweden and Finland has traditionally been more influenced by German suppliers and traditions.

10

Public Procurement in Scandinavia

Oscar Sohl, Head of Public Procurement,
Ekero Kommun

This chapter is primarily about Sweden. However, other Scandin-avian and Nordic countries will be broadly similar.

The market

The Scandinavian market for public procurement amounts to 6000 Bn SEK (Swedish kronor) – approximately £45 billion – a year. In Sweden there are five public sector organisational levels for procurement:

Government	Statlig
County councils	Landsting
Municipalities	Kommuner
The church	Kyrkan
Publicly owned utilities (companies)	Offentligtagda bolag

Government

Government comprises departments, authorities, companies owned by the state, including defence, railways and roads.

County councils

Sweden is divided into 23 county councils or Landsting which also have responsibility for all medical care.

Municipalities

Sweden is divided into 288 municipalities, containing from 3,000 to 1.2 million inhabitants. The municipalities have responsibility for all pre-schools and elderly care.

The church

The church in Sweden has responsibility for all church buildings.

Public owned utilities (companies)

In all three levels there are utilities owned by the government, counties or the municipalities. There are 1,500 in Sweden. These companies also follow the directives for public procurement.

Structure of purchasing within the organisational levels

Most purchasing is decentralised to the appropriate organisational level, size of which will depend on the volumes of purchases. Some purchasing departments will be only part time.

Co-operation

It is quite common for authorities to issue tenders jointly. This means that, for example, four or five municipalities join together in a group in order to offer tenders. This is to increase volume and to simplify the work.

Legal aspects – Swedish Public Procurement Act (LOU)

All countries in Scandinavia follow the EU directives for public purchasing. All the Scandinavian countries have either an act of public procurement or directives.

In Sweden, for example, Parliament decided to implement the Swedish Public Procurement Act (LOU) two years before that country joined the European Union.

Most procurement is carried out according to the Act, including advertising in the official *Journal of the European Commission*, when the value of the goods or services are over the threshold of about 1,700,000 SEK (approximately £130,000 – this follows the EU threshold of 200,000 ecu for supply contracts. There are other thresholds for other types of contract. The thresholds, expressed in ecu, will be the same as in the UK). This means that companies throughout the EU are welcome to bid. Many invitations to tender under this threshold also appear in the special magazines for public procurement.

The effects of the Swedish Public Procurement Act (LOU)

It is disappointing that Sweden's entry into the EU has not raised the amount of foreign tendering for Swedish public procurement. There are many opportunities for foreign companies to join the competition in Sweden and all are welcome to bid. Most of the public purchasers are waiting for the opportunity to do business with other countries this way and not only through agents.

Communication with the purchasers

There are a number of ways of communicating with the public purchasing departments: via the Internet, through various associations, through embassies and through relevant journals and magazines.

By Internet
Many organisations have their own homepage on the Internet, which includes advertisements for tender invitations.

Associations
The following associations can provide the addresses to all public purchase departments:

Sweden:
SOI: Sveriges Offentliga Inkopare (Swedish Public Purchasers)
Tel: +46 16 51 86 60

Denmark:
IKA
Tel: +45 96 117043

Iceland:
Reykjavik Purchasing Centre
Tel: +354 552 58 00

Norway:
NIMA
Tel: +47 22 37 97 10

British embassies
The embassies are a good point of contact, especially in Sweden. The purchasing department sends some of its invitations to tender to the commercial section at the British embassy hoping to find new suppliers.

Magazines and papers
There are a number of magazines and papers where invitations to tender are advertised: *Affarer* (Business) is the Swedish SOI's own magazine. Interested companies can either subscribe or advertise. For information call SOI's office on +46 16 51 86 60; *Andbudsjournalen* and *Anbud och inkop* are two public procurement magazines specialising in advertising for tender invitations under the threshold value.

Most purchasing department officers speak English.

Company/tenderer expectations

It is quite common for authorities to use agreements that last for two or three years. One reason for this is decentralisation of organisations where the volume decision is taken by the school or the daycare centre. It is important, therefore, to have a good distribution system, a wide variety of goods and the ability to meet the purchaser's delivery requirements.

Most small municipalities do not have their own warehouses which means that companies need to have both good distribution and their own warehouse facilities.

Part 3

Accessing the Market

11

Sources of Information and Support

Department of Trade and Industry

The DTI offers a number of areas of support and information including the Business Europe Desk – for telephone support – Export Explorer, Export Promoters to help individual exporters and trade missions, and the Export Market Information Centre, a comprehensive export library.

Business Europe Desk

There is now a single telephone number for all enquiries regarding exports to Europe:

Tel: 0171 215 8885
Fax: 0171 215 8884

Export Explorer

Export Explorer comes in two tailormade packages: Market Explorer and Trade Fair Explorer. The purpose of Market Explorer is to give potential exporters their first taste of a possible export market and focuses on those countries which offer the best opportunities for 'first timers': these are the Republic of Ireland, the Benelux countries and the Nordic countries. Trade Fair Explorer concentrates on some of the world's great marketplaces – the international trade fairs in France, Germany, Italy and Spain. This gives firms the opportunity to see at first hand the marketplace for their products to find out who's selling what, who's buying, and what other British firms are doing without the cost of exhibiting.

Joining Export Explorer will cost just £99. That includes all the hands-on help and support provided by the DTI, plus briefings, information and administration. Travel and accommodation are extra, but there will be special deals offering excellent value on transport and hotels.

The Export Explorer visits themselves will be organised by Business Links, trade associations and other local organisations with support from DTI. Further information about Export Explorer can be obtained by telephoning 0171 215 8885 or by fax on 0171 215 8884.

Participating in Market Explorer

Before your Market Explorer visit you will get:

- a pre-visit meeting with your visit organiser;
- briefing on the country you are visiting;
- a summary of the local market for your product/service;
- a list of named contacts.

On your Market Explorer visit you will get:

- travel with a group of like-minded exporters;
- an experienced exporter on hand to advise throughout the visit;
- help in making appointments should you need it;
- constant back-up from our Foreign and Commonwealth Office commercial team.

After your Market Explorer visit you will get:

- follow-up debriefing with your visit organiser and advice on your next steps;
- information about export opportunities and help to build on your first visit.

For information on Market Explorer telephone 0171 215 8885 or fax on 0171 215 8884.

Export promoters

Tom Burnham is the DTI Export Promoter for the Nordic countries. He can be contacted on tel and fax 01835 830 758.

EMIC – Export Market Information Centre

EMIC is a free 'self-service' library and research facility provided by the DTI to enable you to research export markets. EMIC aims to provide you with market information for all overseas countries and holds an unrivalled selection of statistical, marketing and contact information.

It also holds information about business opportunities arising from the funding of multilateral development agencies, such as the World Bank. This information was formerly held in the DTI's World Aid Section.

EMIC is one of a range of overseas trade services which offers assistance to exporters. If you want further advice on the information you find in EMIC, or guidance on how to trade and do business in each country, they will be happy to refer you to the experts in the DTI's country desks. Many of the country desks have export promoters, private sector secondees to the DTI, who have specialist knowledge of their markets.

Export Market Information Centre
Kingsgate House
66–74 Victoria Street
London SW1E 6SW.
Tel: 0171 215 5444/5
Fax: 0171 215 4231

Admission
Exporters and their representatives, market researchers and consultants can use the Centre free of charge and without prior appointment. Recorded information about EMIC's opening times is available 24 hours a day, every day of the year. Telephone 0171 215 5444/5 and select the relevant option to hear about EMIC.

Students

Business students are welcome but must make an appointment first. As space is limited we have to restrict the number of appointments each day. Students must bring their student ID cards with them when visiting. We recognise that many companies employ students to do research on their behalf. If this is the case, bring a letter of introduction on company stationery setting out the research you are undertaking.

Access for visitors with disabilities

EMIC is located on the first floor of Kingsgate House. If you wish to visit the Centre but are unable to manage the stairs, please ring from the main reception in Kingsgate House and we will arrange for easy access to the Centre via a lift. There is a toilet for visitors with disabilities.

Opening Hours

Monday to Friday 09:00 to 20:00 (last admission at 19:30); Saturdays 09:00 to 17:30 (last admission 17:00).

Local and regional information and support for exporters

Rob Allaker, International Marketing Executive,
County Durham Development Company

Success in exporting lies without doubt in preparation. It is essential to understand the overseas market, the culture and your business targets. Identify market dynamics and learn about the key customers and competitors. Think about your market entry strategy, (direct sales, agent distributor, overseas office etc.). Work on the cost implications to pricing and the benefits which your product have over locally manufactured products. Much of the background information required will be already available to you at little or no cost via the DTI Business Europe Desk and British Embassy Commercial Sections in your potential export markets.

In addition support and information are available from a variety of local economic development organisations (EDOs) which include regional development organisations, business links, chambers of commerce as well as county and district council economic development departments.

Many of these agencies have direct involvement in overseas markets either via a permanent office or by regular market visits to strategically important countries or regions. The more professional of these will also have developed a close working relationship with the relevant embassies and overseas desks of the DTI.

Trade missions

Many regional organisations also arrange or participate in a variety of trade missions. Some, and arguably the more effective of these, tend to be sector specific and closely aligned to the industrial sectors of importance to the appropriate overseas market. This type of sectoral focus also tends to be of greater appeal to small manufacturers who demand the opportunity to network widely through participation. Value for money is critical to SMEs and the more relevant appointments which can be accommodated, the better the chance of success.

Financial subsidies

A further means of assistance lies in financial subsidies. While many trade missions already benefit from DTI support, others do not. In both instances, however, there may be scope for additional financial help from local agencies – usually county and district economic development companies. It is always worth making enquiries to your local EDO, business link or export development counsellor. Bear in mind that in order to qualify, it may be necessary to apply before committing to travel. Financial assistance tends to be higher and more readily available in areas in receipt of regional grants and EU regional support.

Sources of information and contacts

In the North East of England local EDOs meet regularly under the North East Export Forum system. At this meeting such organisations (Chambers of Commerce, Northern Development Company, Business Links, Development Companies, etc.) can update others on export events under preparation or organisation.

Finally, many locally based EDOs will themselves seek to provide improved links with DTI desks and overseas offices. It is a requirement for British embassy commercial staff to undertake a UK-based duty tour mid-way through their assignments. These duty tours last one–two weeks and the officers do like to travel throughout the UK to build up their own knowledge of the home market as well as to share their own experience as widely as possible. Local agencies often, therefore, host country- or sector-specific seminars which could be attended by DTI export trade promoters, locally based overseas trade service representatives, country desk representatives as well as the commercial officers themselves. For the first-time or inexperienced SME exporter the ability to reach such a range of potential sources of help is invaluable.

The rewards available to successful exporters are proportional to the risk. The risk, however, can be reduced significantly by preliminary desk research in partnership with local, UK based and overseas representatives of EDOs, the DTI country desks and embassy commercial sections.

Case Study I

In early 1998 the County Durham Development Company organised a small trade mission to Finland, focused exclusively on the electronics sector. Five SMEs attended, including one from a neighbouring county and were joined in Finland by a further electronics manufacturer from the Midlands. Meetings, events and visits were prepared in conjunction with the British Embassy Finland, the DTI Finland Desk, the Finnish Electronics Manufacturing Association and included attendance at the electrometal Interprise event in Turku (for more information about Interprise see Harley Atherton's article on Trade Visits and Events).

As a result of the highly specific focus of the visit, every one of the businesses left having exceeded its own targets and expectations. Outstanding success was due to the way in which CDDC utilised its knowledge of the local manufacturing companies in its area, coupled with an excellent network of contacts within Finland and the DTI.

Role of Business Links in Export Promotion

Background

The aim of Overseas Trade Services (OTS) is to support UK Business abroad. At the local level Business Links provide the primary access point to the OTS for Small and Medium Enterprises (SMEs) in England and Wales. The DTI currently has 109 staff seconded from Government Offices in Business Links, most of whom are dedicated to delivering export services, and is providing funding towards the costs of Export Development Counsellors (EDCs), recruited from the private sector. Eighty-two EDCs are now in place, with the task of working with SMEs to help them develop effective export strategies. They work as a member of an integrated International Trade Team with: the DTI secondees, Chambers of Commerce and other partner bodies.

Complementary Roles of Business Links & OTS

There are considerable benefits for UK business in the provision of an integrated export service at the local level, bringing together all available sources of help and advice including those available from OTS, and placed in an integrated system for advising local companies about their needs generally. The Business Links network offers the prospect of improved exporting performance by British business.

OTS has a remit to:

• provide help and advice relating to specific overseas markets;
• carry out promotional activities abroad;
• help firms integrate export opportunities effectively in their growth and development strategies.

Business Links, based on their understanding of the needs of individual firms, are best placed to advise companies on whether and how exporting can assist their overall performance, and help customers make the best use of Overseas Trade Services. This support will include:

- market information and promotional support;
- one-to-one help, advice and counselling, including an export 'health check' to help assess whether exporting is in the client's best interests;
- strategic advice to help the client plan and implement an export strategy;
- assistance to ensure that the client has access to the most appropriate expert advice on exporting from partners, other local national providers, including seamless access to Overseas Trade Services;
- follow up to the use of these services, in order to establish the extent to which they meet client needs and what further advice and help the client might want.

Information and support from British embassies in Nordic countries

Ole H. Christensen, Commercial Officer,
British Embassy, Copenhagen

- *For £100 your embassy abroad will perform up to four hours of research.* This is the typical cost for a 'cold' list of potential agents. That is the time it takes to identify, check and type such a list. In certain circumstances a 'cold' list may suffice, but it frequently happens that clients have bought such a list only to find that several of the agents (or distributors) listed already represent their direct competitors. Obviously this sort of list is what is needed only if the product concerned is one to be sold directly to overseas customers without the use of middlemen, or if the exporter is absolutely certain that he has no competitors.
- *At £200 your embassy abroad will perform up to eight hours of research.* That will buy you two 'cold' lists and much of what has already been mentioned applies to this service too. Eight hours is usually not enough time to do in-depth research.
- *At £300 your embassy abroad will perform up to twelve hours of research.* That gives the necessary time to do a detailed and thorough job for you. Here we start researching the market potential for your particular product using the published statistics. The key to this is the CCCN No (Harmonised System

Code). Please make sure to include it in your enquiry. If you do not know the number, the Customs and Excise office can help.

- *For £600 your embassy abroad will perform up to 24 hours of research.* This gives us even more time to do the detailed and meticulous job already described.

We try to ascertain whether your competitors are represented locally and, if so, by whom. So please be sure to include a list of your competitors, both UK and foreign, in your enquiry. Then we make a list of potential agents, but now it is no longer a 'cold' list. Now it is a collection of names of agents/distributors not already representing a competitor (though they may, of course, be selling complementary products).

Finally we check if there are any standards, rules and regulations with which your products must comply.

As part of the Export Representative Service, we usually include a condensed version of the research already described but here we also undertake to approach the potential agents/ distributors on your behalf, using your literature etc. Their response forms part of our final report, along with an overseas status report on each of those firms which expressed positive interest in representing you. The latter provides a solid and detailed profile of the prospective agent/distributor.

Along with these reports many British embassies will include several 'freebies', such as information on the current economy, notes on how to do business locally, business etiquette, travel arrangements etc.

- *For £1,200 your embassy abroad will perform over 48 hours of research, and each additional 24 hours work costs £600.* It is rare that research in a small country requires that length of time.

We undertake other relevant services and can thus assist with a programme arranging service; in-market help service; seminar organisation service. There is a minimum charge – up to two hours' work at £80 and hourly thereafter at £40.

Case Study 1

In May 1995 Howard Graham of Futuro Limited, manufacturers of high class diamond jewellery into wholesale and retail markets, commissioned a list of potential Norwegian customers from the British Embassy in

Oslo at a cost of £100. He considers it one of the best investments that he has ever made. They were then able to use this to cold call on the potential customers. They won a substantial order from one of the contacts on the list and their business grew from there.

Having established themselves in Norway, they were then able to expand into other Scandinavian markets, again with the help of the local embassies. Today the region accounts for about 10 per cent of sales, although the current strength of the pound is reducing their profit margins and stopping them developing new lines in the region.

They have found Scandinavians very easy to do business with and very willing to see new suppliers. They are friendly and often easier to deal with than Britons and he now has many friends in the region.

British embassies

Denmark
British Embassy
Kastelsvej 36
DK-2100 Copenhagen O
Tel: +45 35 266375
Fax: +45 35 445246

Finland
British Embassy
Itainen Puistotie 17, 00140 Helsinki
Tel: +358 9 2286 5100
Fax: +358 9 2286 5262

Iceland
British Embassy
Laufasvegur 31, PO Box 460, Reykjavik
Tel: +354 550 5100/1/2
Fax: +354 550 5105

Norway
British Embassy
Thomas Heftyesgate 8, 0264 Oslo
Tel: +47 23 13 27 00
Fax: +47 23 13 27 05

Sweden
British Embassy
Skarpögatan 6–8, Box 27819, S-115 93, Stockholm
Tel: +46 8 671 9000
Fax: +46 8 662 9989

British Consulate General
Drottninggatan 63, 41107, Gothenburg
Tel: +46 31 13 13 27
Fax: +46 31 13 56 85

12

Trade Visits and Events: Help from the European Union for Exporters

Harley Atherton, T F Marketing

EU initiatives to help SMEs

To small and medium-sized companies (SMEs) the European Union often appears as a provider of help and assistance, but usually to someone else. However, there are two EU initiatives that are becoming increasingly popular and are available to all.

These are EUROPARTENARIAT and INTERPRISE. They are both based on the same principle, which is to bring SMEs together from all over Europe for pre-arranged business-to-business meetings all at one venue. There was a EUROPARTENARIAT in Apeldoorn in the Netherlands in June 1998 with further events planned in Valencia, Vienna and Bavaria (the contact is the British Chambers of Commerce on 01203 694484). It is for companies from any industry and succeeds because of scale – literally thousands of companies participate while INTERPRISE is confined to one industry sector – normally around 150 companies will take part from perhaps ten different countries from the EU or associated countries.

How INTERPRISE works

The INTERPRISE organisers will probably be a consortium of the local chambers, regional government and the local representatives of national government. They select a suitable industry sector, usually that one is applicable to their region, and start to recruit local companies. These companies can be interested in talking to their overseas visitors about joint venture activity, technology transfer, sub-contracting and, of course, buying and selling.

The organisers then select partners in other EU countries that are most relevant. The job of these partners is to recruit around fifteen companies from their country to join the INTERPRISE. In the UK the partner could be my organisation, T F Marketing, or sometimes a regional European Information Centre (EIC).

The companies travelling from the UK and the other countries would send in their details together with a specification of their aims and ambitions in attending the event. Typical aims would be to sell their product range, to source parts or to look for co-operation in research and development. All these details are then printed in a catalogue that is circulated by the organisers to all participating companies, which then decide who they wish to meet during the event. At the same time companies from other countries, or indeed the UK, book meetings with them. These meetings usually last between half and three-quarters of an hour which is quite long enough to establish whether or not there is a possibility of doing business. As all the meetings are in the same venue it is possible for a company to have as many as twenty meetings in the two days. In our experience over 50 per cent of these meetings have led to further contact.

The social events in the evening, usually hosted by the local region or city, are just as valuable. Talking to people in the same business even if you had not planned to meet them often produces surprising results.

The support that companies receive from the organisers and their own national partners means that INTERPRISE is an ideal opportunity for first-time exporters although perhaps the major advantage for any company is that it has around 150 potential partners or customers from maybe ten different countries all under one roof. It is a most cost- and time-effective way of doing business.

T F Marketing is an organisation specialising in working in the UK as one of the partners for INTERPRISE events, particularly those in Scandinavia. They have produced British groups to attend INTERPRISE events in Finland on selling to Russia, sustainable energy, water and air treatment and wood and paper industry suppliers. In Sweden the product area was suppliers of products to the disabled and elderly and in Iceland it was, not surprisingly, fish and fish processing. Another INTERPRISE for the fishing and seafood industry took place in Tromso in Norway in May 1998. In Seinajoki, Finland, in June 1998 the chosen industry was wood processing and furniture. There are others to follow in Finland later that year on telecommunications, and in Sweden on educational supplies.

13

Business Culture in Scandinavia

Bob Mason

"They like to be treated as individuals!"

It is very tempting to lump all the Nordic countries (Norway, Sweden, Denmark, Finland and Iceland) together. They have similar climates and cultures and their histories are intrinsically linked. However, they all have their own identities and quirks and deserve to be respected accordingly. They like to be treated as individuals.

All the Nordic countries have small populations sparsely distributed through large geographical areas. This has historically resulted in a breed of independent people, with strong opinions and a culture of self-reliance. They also like to be treated as individuals.

Having said this, there are many common threads that make it easy to do business across the region.

Organisations

Companies tend to have 'flat management structures' and the thinking is much less hierarchical than in the UK, hence staff are empowered to make decisions and this is expected of visitors too.

Meetings are well structured and professional presentations and material are expected.

The working day is quite tightly controlled: work is for work, free time is for the family. This means that business discussions cannot automatically extend beyond the allotted time and business entertainment needs to be carefully planned in advance.

People

People are very direct and usually want to get straight to the point – this can appear aggressive. They are slow to make friends, but once you have established a personal friendship, you have a loyal friend for life. They will dress informally for work. However, they will usually expect a Briton to dress like a Briton should – i.e. reasonably formally, at least for initial meetings, although you will usually find that they will be on first name terms very quickly.

Language is not a problem as English is widely spoken across the region and there are long-standing associations with Britain which make us well received.

They are renowned as technology freaks, for example, with some of the highest levels of mobile phone and Internet usage in the world.

The people are wealthy, have a high standard of living and expect high quality, reliable goods and services. However, because of this apparent conformity across the region, it will help to have some flavour of the individual characteristics of each market.

Denmark

- Danes are very independent; of farming and sea-going ancestry, they are natural traders. They work for companies that are small by European standards, where staff are empowered to make decisions.
- English is widely spoken, but in southern Jutland the first foreign language is likely to be German.
- There is a long history of conflict with Sweden.
- Denmark is the most continental of all the Nordic countries.

Finland

- The Finns are much more serious. Already bi-lingual in Finnish and Swedish, the level of English is not as consistently high as the rest of the region.

- They are more reserved and words are only used when necessary – silence is part of conversation.
- As a consequence they are arguably better negotiators as we tend to fill silence with meaningless words.
- They have a long history of trading with Russia.

Iceland

- The most isolated of the Nordic countries and very dependent on imports. Most importing is carried out by family firms who, for security, represent a diverse range of principals.
- Companies are conservative and jealously guard their business information.
- Of recent years, there are few British businesses that feel they can justify the cost of visiting Iceland. The consequence of this is that those who do visit are guaranteed a warm welcome – as long as they have good products at a reasonable price.
- Be prepared to discuss fish and compliment them on the quality of their lamb. Be prepared for lots of weather too.
- As Iceland is a former colony of Denmark, it is better not to treat the country as an extension of your Danish business.

Norway

- Norway also has a conservative business culture. People are generally more cautious than the Swedes and less inclined to small talk. There is a very strong inclination to consensus management within companies.
- There is a long history to Norway's relationship with Sweden (its union with Sweden only came to an end in 1905) and it is better not to give the impression that your business in Norway is an adjunct to that in Sweden.
- The Norwegians are proud of their history and culture, and the progress that has been achieved through harnessing the oil and gas resources of the North Sea.
- Whaling is a sensitive subject and should be avoided.

Sweden

- Sweden is the dominant economic, industrial and military force in the region. This means that the Swedes tend to be envied, while they look down on the others as rural neighbours.

- Sweden has a large number of multi-national companies and there is a more corporate nature to many businesses. However, this is counterbalanced by the consensus approach to the running of companies.

Ten personal tips to help you throughout the Nordic region

1. Do arrive for meetings punctually or notify in advance if you are going to be late.
2. Do state times using the 24-hour clock (this avoids confusion over the meaning of 'half-five').
3. Do give a firm handshake on arrival and departure.
4. If you are a smoker, respect no-smoking areas, which are increasingly company wide.
5. Expect to carry out all business in English (if you do have any material translated, it must be done very accurately and professionally to avoid appearing a joke).
6. Do not be embarrassed to talk about price and payment, and note payment is normally prompt and usually interest is charged and paid if payments are late.
7. Do not be surprised by 'straight talking' – it is normal practice to be direct.
8. Do not make a promise or enter into an agreement if you fear you cannot fulfil it – they prefer to know where they stand and will respect you for honesty.
9. Ensure that any trade material sent in advance is good quality – do not forward photocopies or price lists amended in manuscript.
10. Be prepared to be offered alcoholic drinks for lunch or dinner, but it is quite acceptable to request mineral water or 'light' beer, especially given the very strict drink-drive laws; if invited to a private home, it is normal to take a bouquet of flowers or box of chocolates for your hostess.

However, do not be put off by all this advice – keep an open mind, learn by experience and above all else enjoy winning some business.

14

Telecommunications and IT

Clive Smithers, County Durham On Line

It Still Does Nothing, or I Smell Dollars Now.

These were two contrasting suggestions of the commercial potential of Integrated Speech and Data Services (ISDN) on its introduction by BT. They also represent the two possible attitudes of potential exporters to the benefits of using modern information and communications technology (often referred to as ICT, informatics or telematics).

These technologies have much to offer to some businesses in the right circumstances. Business, cultural and human factors mean that they present particular advantages to the support and development of export business with the Nordic countries.

The Nordic countries

Within the Nordic countries there is a prevailing culture which accepts the use of these technologies as an everyday occurrence. The size and remoteness of the area, with relatively low population and scattered settlements, has led to the provision of a high-quality telecommunications infrastructure. Access to learning, leisure opportunities and even medical diagnosis is delivered through these technologies; it is then a natural step to accept them within the world of business.

DTI research shows high levels of cellular phone use, personal computer usage in the workforce, and low costs of mobile and traditional telephony. Business people often fall into the category known as 'early adopters' – people who will quickly see the advantages of technological advances and their potential applications.

Other factors include the high level of competence in English speaking and a high level of electronic procurement for public purchasing and contracts. This has encouraged the use of electronic data interchange (EDI) and e-mail systems by companies operating in this marketplace. The region contains leading companies in the ICT sector, including Nokia, Ericsson and Telia.

In general then, there is a culture and a business conducive to doing business electronically.

Business applications

What applications can help business to take advantage of this situation? While technology can make work tasks cheaper, faster or more effective, this is always subject to business and human factors. For example, video conferencing can be a very good way of developing and maintaining existing customer relationships; but it cannot substitute for the need for personal contact at the beginning of such a relationship. With this in mind, the key opportunities which effective use of ICT can offer exporters include:

- access to new markets;
- live product demonstrations to customers or agents;
- provision of technical and sales support;
- a global storefront, including company promotion, on-line catalogues and ordering, and secure transactions;
- closer links to agents or direct relationships with customers;
- customer support and relationship management;
- cost savings;
- competitive advantage (arising from all these factors).

Key technologies are:

- World Wide Web (WWW) and Internet applications (see Chapter 20);
- electronic mail (e-mail);
- video conferencing.

E-mail

E-mail provides the opportunity to send messages to anyone in the world with an e-mail address. It operates at local call charge rates, wherever in the world you are sending the message, and you can work off line until you need to send the message. You can also attach and send documents or spreadsheets, which can then be worked on by the recipient.

E-mail is fast, but how quickly it is received may depend on the working routine of the recipient – if they only switch their computer on once a day a fax may be quicker. Many people can access their e-mail address from a laptop computer or other device, so can receive messages wherever they are.

Video conferencing

Video conferencing can speed up discussions and negotiations, reduce the time spent on meetings, remove travelling time and costs, and enhance the effectiveness of meetings. A variety of systems is available, from desktop systems operating on your personal computer to full room systems.

Most systems will be compatible for voice and picture. Video conferencing also offers opportunities to share data in real time – people at each location can work on the same document at the same time, with voice communication, all mediated through the system.

This can only serve as a brief introduction to the use of these technologies.

If you are interested in further information, the DTI has published a series of award winning guides as part of the ISI Programme for Business. In this series 'How technology can work for you', three of the six titles are e-mail and fax, video conferencing, and the Internet. These are highly recommended.

As part of the ISI programme there is a network of local support centres, one in each business link area.

You can contact the ISI Programme for Business by dialling the Infoline on 0345 15 2000; e-mailing to info@isi.gov.uk; or visiting the web site at http://www.isi.gov.uk.

15

Travelling to and within the Nordic Countries

Graham Wason

Introduction

Getting there

The Nordic Countries (comprising the three Scandinavian countries of Denmark, Norway and Sweden, together with Finland and Iceland) have since modern times been the most expensive region of Europe to visit and in which to travel around. The airways have been dominated by expensive national carriers (notably Scandinavian Airline System (SAS), owned jointly by the governments of Denmark, Norway and Sweden) with monopolistic positions and high operating costs.

The price differential with other parts of Europe has narrowed over the past two decades as other carriers, including budget operators, have entered the market, and as the economies of these countries have faced stiffer conditions. An apex return to the capital cities of the region can cost as little as £100 (plus taxes). There was a set-back to this trend caused when Air Europe (part of the International Leisure Group) went bust in the mid-1980s. And, with Debonair ceasing its operations to Copenhagen in 1998 due to high landing fees and servicing costs, and the increasing burden of environmental costs which are particularly heavy in the Nordic region, the price differential might not narrow any further. Prices are also being squeezed upwards by the introduction and subsequent increases in departure taxes.

As with most other destinations, where the independent business person is able to extend a visit over a Saturday night, travel costs can be much lower. Indeed, it can be cheaper to take your partner, stay over the weekend, and include accommodation in a package for two, than to pay a single, business class fare.

If you need to take samples or excess baggage with you, and are not time constrained, consider taking the car by sea. The ferry ships between the UK and Denmark and Sweden are excellent, giving you in effect the opportunity for a 24-hour cruise each way.

Travelling around

Geographically, the Nordic countries span a vast region. Surface communications are hampered in the south by the many islands and fjords, and the terrain becomes increasingly inhospitable and sparsely populated to the north. But standards of facilities and reliability are high, for example, on the many ferries. Other facilities, such as hotels and restaurants, trim labour-intensive services as much as possible, due to high wage and social costs.

If you are visiting a number of destinations within the region, it might be worth buying an SAS AirPass. The Scandinavian AirPass starts at £50 for a one-way flight and goes up to £300 for six flights within and between Denmark, Norway, Sweden and Finland. The Baltic AirPass includes selected destinations in Russia and the Baltic States. Airpasses must be purchased together with an international ticket.

Driving in the Nordic region is generally hassle free and, with quiet roads, often a pleasant change from the UK. International rules and regulations generally apply. All countries of the region require you to carry a warning triangle, and most require seatbelts to be worn in the rear as well as front seats and children must wear appropriate restraints. Most countries require the use of dipped headlamps at all times, even in bright sunshine in the middle of summer. Headlamp adjusters are necessary if you take a UK vehicle. Alcohol restrictions are severe, particularly in Norway and Sweden. Speed limits are generally 50 km/hr in towns, 70 to 90 km/hr on normal roads and 90 to 110 on motorways. Most international car hire firms are represented throughout the Nordic region.

Denmark

Getting there

Most international flights go to Copenhagen Airport (Kastrup), with services operated by SAS, British Airways, Maersk and British Midland. Prices and services are comparable, but change frequently and it is always worth shopping around, especially if you have flexibility over dates and timings. Some regional UK airports have direct flights (Manchester, Newcastle, Edinburgh, Glasgow, Aberdeen) and, in Jutland, there are direct flights from Heathrow to Aarhus (SAS) and from Gatwick to Billund (Maersk). Most flights are of around one and a half hours' duration.

For surface travel, there is an excellent ferry service from Harwich to Esbjerg (Jutland), which takes 20 hours and sails several times per week. Rail connections are also possible, via ferry services to Esbjerg, Hook of Holland or Ostend. The fastest rail service is on Eurostar to Brussels, then onward to Copenhagen.

Travelling around

Virtually every regional airport can be reached within an hour's flying time from Copenhagen. However, as there are relatively few major cities in Denmark, regional airports sometimes serve several towns and may therefore involve relatively long ground connections.

Railways are operated by the state rail company, DSB, and are frequent, fast and efficient. Some express trains require prebooking.

All islands are connected by ferries which are usually frequent and highly efficient and reliable. Some routes use high-speed vessels.

Road connections will be greatly improved in the summer of 1998 with the opening of the bridge over the Great Belt, thus making Copenhagen accessible directly from mainland Europe.

Hotels are generally of good standard but not cheap. Hotels that are members of HORESTA (the Danish Hotel, Restaurant and

Tourist Employers' Association) participate in a voluntary grading system (one to five stars). Danish Inn Holidays (Dansk Kroferie) sell 'cheques' which give discounts of 10 to 25 per cent at 85 inns and hotels (£60 to £80 per night for two, bed and breakfast, in a room with bathroom).

The Faeroe Islands

Although of more interest to the leisure than the business traveller, these Danish islands, located between Scotland and Iceland, are served by daily Maersk or Atlantic Airways flights from Copenhagen, and less frequent services from Aarhus and Billund (flying time, two and a quarter hours).

Greenland

There are some business opportunities in Greenland, the world's largest island, still part of the Danish Kingdom, home rule since 1979 notwithstanding. There are scheduled services to four international airports by Grønlandsfly or Travelling Greenland Air. Hotels are generally modern and comfortable.

Norway

Getting There

Oslo is the international hub although international flights are available to some more northerly destinations. Flight times range from just under two to about three hours. British Airways and SAS have flights to Oslo several times a day from Heathrow and Gatwick, as well as services to Stavanger. SAS also has services from Manchester to Oslo and Aberdeen to Stavanger. In the summer SAS flies to Tromsø. Braathens operate most days to Oslo from London and Newcastle, and have occasional direct flights to Bergen, Stavanger and Trondheim. A summer service connects Jersey and Oslo. British Midland fly Heathrow to Oslo, and Air UK have services from Aberdeen, Stansted and Norwich. Other services are provided by Coast Air (Aberdeen to Haugesund and Bergen) and Ryanair (Stansted to Oslo (south) Torp airport).

Ferry services are provided by Color Line (Newcastle–Stavanger–Haugesund–Bergen) and Scandinavian Seaways (Harwich to Gothenburg in Sweden). There are additional summer sailings.

Travelling around

Most domestic business travel is by air due to Norway's length and difficult terrain. Consequently the country is well served by some 50 airports and airfields. The main domestic carriers are SAS, Braathens and Widerøe.

Ferries and express boats link the coastal towns. Most notable is the Norwegian Coastal Express that covers the 2,500 nautical miles of coastline and 34 ports in 11 days.

Norwegian State Railways (NSB) connect the main cities. Onward travel is usually provided by bus. Towards the coast, the scenery is stunning but the terrain makes journey times long.

Hotels vary considerably in style, but quality is consistently good. Book through a travel agent as the Norwegian Tourist Board does not provide a booking service. The mid-June to mid-August high season can get very busy. The main hotel operators include Rasdisson SAS and Scandic. Other affiliations include Best Western, and Rica Hotels. English-style B&B is becoming popular in Norway. It can be booked on the day in the local tourist office, or at the central railway station in Oslo. There is a B&B guidebook called *Rom i Norge*, which is available through Norsc Holidays in the UK, tel 01297 560033.

Sweden

Getting there

There are four international airports in Sweden. There are five flights daily to Stockholm from Heathrow and two from Gatwick. Flights also depart from Edinburgh, Manchester and Stansted. Flight times are two to three hours.

Ferries depart for Gothenburg twice weekly from Harwich and once weekly from Newcastle (around 24 hours). There are regular services by sea and rail from Denmark to various points in Sweden.

Travelling around

SAS operates to 21 destinations in Sweden. A number of other operators run domestic services.

Swedish trains are excellent. The X2000 high-speed train has radio and music channel outlets by all seats, and meals served at your seat in first class or a bistro in standard class. A cinema coach is provided on night trains. Seat reservations are always advisable and often compulsory.

Sweden has a wide variety of hotels. Most include a generous buffet breakfast. Several groups, such as Reso, offer 'cheques' to encourage your loyalty as you travel around. There is a comprehensive listing of hotels called 'Hotels in Sweden' which is available free from the Swedish Travel and Tourism Council in London.

Finland

Getting there

Finland's national airline, Finnair, has flights from London both direct and via Stockholm. Journey time is three to three and a half hours. There is also a service to Turku via Stockholm.

Helsinki–Vantaa Airport lies some 20 kilometres north of the city. There is a separate business flight terminal for private flights and air taxis. There is a 35-minute bus journey to the main railway station between two and four times per hour.

Helsinki is well served by ferries within the Baltic region, and by rail to Russia.

Travelling around

Most domestic services are provided by Finnair. The most northerly airports are over two hours away.

The southern half of the country is well served by an electrified rail network, operated by VR ltd, the Finnish Railways network. Oulo, at the limit of the electrification, is some six and a half hours away.

Hotels are mostly of good standard, with rooms having bath or shower, TV, telephone and mini-bar. There is usually a sauna, and many have a swimming pool. Sokos is the largest national hotel chain, with some 40 hotels in 26 cities. Another well-represented Finnish group is Arctia. Best Western and Scandic both have a reasonable distribution of hotels. The Restel Hotel Group brands hotels as Cumuluis, Rantasipi or Ramada.

Iceland

Getting there

Icelandair and British Airways fly via Glasgow to Keflavik Airport, 31 miles from Reykjavik. Flights are very expensive – a 3-day excursion fare costs around £670 excluding taxes.

Most major hotels have buses which meet international flights at the airport. There is a charge of about £5. Taxis cost nearer £50, although they can be cheaper if booked in advance (contact Iceland Tourist Board in London).

Travelling around

There are few large settlements outside Reykjavik. If you need to go any distance, Icelandair operate domestic flights. For shorter distances, a rented car might suffice – the major international car hire chains are all represented. Maximum speed limit is 90 km/hr. Weather conditions can be hazardous off the main coast road. There are buses serving local towns, but no trains.

Part 4

Business Development

16

A Sales Presence

Gerry O'Brien

Direct sales and support presence

Almost all small and medium-sized companies who break into a market do so via agents and distributors in the first instance. However, there does come a time when a decision has to be made as to whether the exporter should set up a direct sales and support presence in the overseas market. In Scandinavia it is much more common for Swedish and German companies to have direct sales presence than it is for British companies.

The attractions of a direct sales subsidiary are:

- it works exclusively for the principal and carries no conflicting agencies (however, if you do not have a full range of products it might be an advantage to use an agent or distributor with complementary products);
- it concentrates totally on the sale of the principal's goods with no conflicting interests;
- it shows the customer that the UK exporter is totally committed to the market;
- it can reduce travelling for UK-based sales staff;
- it can give a better understanding of the market and the needs of the local customers;
- it can reduce the need for UK-based interpretation services.

However there is a downside:

- it can be expensive to set up and run an overseas office;
- it will still need monitoring from the UK (in the early days probably even so more than a distributor);
- there can be complicated tax and profit repatriation issues (see Chapter 26)
- recruiting staff can be difficult (see Chapter 40);
- if you are exporting to more than one country you may have to consider whether to set up subsidiaries in each:
  - there are questions of national rivalry and Danes for instance might prefer to deal with London rather than Stockholm. It is of interest that for many years IBM's Nordic marketing centre was based in Chiswick in London rather than in any particular Nordic country;
  - air connections are good and in the main cheap from the UK; you might find it easier to get to your destination from here than from a regional office.

Setting up in business

In the UK we are used to being able to start up a business simply and easily, often without any form of registration or formal qualification. On the continent this is generally a more formal affair. Setting up a sales organisation, or any other form of business entity, will have to follow different rules in different countries. However, the basic procedures are the same across the Nordic region.

You can be represented by one or more individuals who are residents of the European Economic Area (EU plus Norway, Iceland and Liechtenstein) and they can trade under your name. You may have to register that trade name. If you do this you are in effect running a branch office which just happens to be in a foreign country. Usually a branch office will not be regarded as an independent entity but as a division of its head office, who will be responsible for its liabilities.

It is also possible to set up a representative office. This can have the advantage of completely escaping local taxation and regulation. However, it may not conclude any sales or service. It is there merely to support the local organisation, for instance with marketing help.

Where you have established dealers or agents, a representative office may be a good way to support them with a longer term view of setting up your own sales organisation.

You may set up a partnership with a local individual or legal entity. Again partnership law will vary from country to country but broadly there are general partnerships where each partner has joint and several liability for its liabilities or limited partnership where a 'sleeping' partner may not have liability. Other regulations will be broadly similar to a sole trader.

If you want to found a limited company there is usually no problem for EEA resident individuals and companies. Broadly speaking, company law will be similar to the UK.

You may have to have a trade permit. Typically this would state the nature of your business, its location and the name and nationality of the applicant. There may be a fee for this. Often you will have to nominate a local resident, who does not have to be a local national, to receive summonses and other notifications. Some trades are regulated and you should check this out, though it would not normally be the case for pure sales outlets – depending, of course, on what you are selling.

Most of the big accountancy firms have free booklets on setting up businesses in individual countries and these are well worth reading. However, you should always get legal advice before setting up any sort of overseas presence. As ever, your overseas British embassy will always be ready to help you get started.

17

Using Agents and Distributors: a Guide for Exporters

Ole H. Christensen, Commercial Officer, British Embassy, Copenhagen (with additional material by The Institute of Export, London)

Agent or distributor?

Most exports pass through the hands of agents or distributors so naturally the emphasis of the DTI export initiatives is on assisting British exporters to find the right ones. But what is the difference between an agent and a distributor?

An agent is a person or company selling in the principal's name from whom he receives a commission.

A distributor sells in his own name, carries stocks etc. and usually gets a favourable discount for his efforts.

Both agent and distributor have one thing in common: not all of their principals are of equal importance to them. Usually the 20:80 rule applies: 20 per cent of the agencies provide 80 per cent of the turnover. In electronics the ratio is typically 10:90. This means that 80 per cent of the agencies carried by the agent share only 20 per cent of his turnover (or one could say his 'interest'). Obviously, many such agencies are of only marginal interest to agents/distributors and they frequently terminate them.

Embassies worldwide are familiar with certain recurring questions:

> My agent is not doing anything for me – should I try to find another one?

> I know we don't visit our agent as often as we should, but what can we do to make him perform better or to concentrate more on our products?

There are no simple answers. Sometimes a UK exporter in this situation may not have realised that a change has taken place in the overseas market concerned. The theory of 'sell to the agent/distributor and let him look after the market' has over many years been giving way to that of 'sell to the customer through the agent/distributor'. This involves investing far more time in supporting the agent/distributor, and this means the export area manager must go out and call on customers together with the agent's/distributor's salesmen. This is expensive but reaps important benefits.

The agent's salesman is only human. He will go out every day calling on those customers who are most likely to order. These may not necessarily be customers interested in your product. But when you go out with the salesman, you train him to sell your products and at the end of the day he will be encouraged to set a sales target for himself. Also the customers will be interested because they can now get answers to all their questions immediately. This means the exporter gets to know the customers and their requirements. And as a bonus the exporter is not automatically back at square one if, for some reason, he must change agents or distributors at a later date. This means that the exporter must see the export market as an extension of his natural market and that is really what it is all about. In many cases, especially inside the European Single Market, the producers of goods and services are already doing all their own sales and marketing, delivery and some service work abroad.

So after the embassy abroad has done what it can and found you an agent/distributor, and you have visited him and made an

agreement, you should write to him and ask him to organise a
visiting schedule to potential key customers, for both you and
members of his sales staff. He will find it very difficult to refuse.
And do not forget that you should have a formal contract with
agents and distributors (see Chapter 35) rather than a few notes
on half the napkin from the dinner at which the agreement was
made. You should try and ensure that UK law will apply to any
dispute. You should also consider specifying alternative dispute
resolution (see Chapter 35).

Failure to have a contract inevitably means that in any dispute
the case will be tried in Denmark, Sweden, Norway, Iceland or
Finland, ie the agents'/distributors' country, and not the UK. This
can be both difficult, time consuming and expensive to win.

Agents

- An agent is a person or company selling in the principal's name
  from whom he receives a commission. He looks after the interests
  of the principal at all times, negotiates on his behalf and gets
  the best possible deal for him.
- It is better to use an agent when the exporter wishes to use local
  distribution channels without having to invest in his own sales
  force.
- An agent can be used for practically every kind of product from
  a capital project to the sale of tin tacks; it all depends on the
  ability of the exporter to deal direct with the buyer and to supply
  the goods in accordance with the terms of the contract.
- He must be well known in the business community and well
  respected; he must be self-motivated and capable of working on
  his own initiative.
- Ensure that the agent understands international trade procedures.
- Avoid agents with too many competing lines which will result in
  insufficient attention being given to your product.
- Take up references on the agent and visit him in his own country
  to ascertain how he operates; he must be continually serviced
  by the exporter with regular visits to ensure that he is doing his
  job well and is motivated properly.

Case Study I

An example of a case that went badly wrong was where the agent took control and the exporter became reactive and not proactive. An agent selling air ventilation equipment recommended that the exporter sue a competitor who had produced a similar product which, in his opinion, infringed the exporter's patent. The exporter did not check out the facts and sued; he subsequently lost the case which cost him a lot of money because he relied too heavily on the opinion of the agent.

Distributors

- A distributor sells in his own name, carries stocks etc. and usually gets a favourable discount for his efforts. He uses his expertise to market and sell the exporter's product at a profit to end users through his established network of wholesale or retail outlets.
- It is better to use a distributor when the exporter wishes to use local distribution channels without having to invest in his own sales force.
- Most consumer goods are suitable for distributorship, e.g. cars, food, sport, electrical goods, photography, and pharmaceuticals. Capital goods are usually sold direct by the exporter to the overseas buyer, often using the services of an agent.
- The key points to look for in choosing a distributor are that it should be an established business, well known in the chosen trade sector; knowledge of the product is vital if regular sales are to be achieved and for the product to find an established place in the market.
- Avoid distributors with too many competing lines which will result in insufficient attention being given to your product. Ensure that good promotion and advertising of the product are available.
- Take up references on the distributor and visit him in his own country to ascertain how he operates; he must be continually serviced by the exporter with regular visits to ensure that he is doing his job well and is motivated properly.

Case Study 2

A case which had gone badly wrong was where the exporter had not received good advice from his distributor regarding the packaging of his product and frozen fish had innocently been packed the same way as cat food. As soon as the packaging was changed, sales immediately picked up.

Case Study 3

A well-known British toiletry and gift company has been exporting to Sweden, Denmark and Norway for about fifteen years. Its Norwegian distributor retired and the company obtained a list of potential new distributors from the DTI/British Embassy at a cost of £100. It appointed a new distributor in 1996. The first year's business was good. However, problems started when the British company went through a period of change, at the same time the previous export manager left and there was a period of some months before a successor was appointed and the level of supervision and monitoring dropped.

Although the company was in the toiletries and gift market its distributor was in the perfumery sector. Unfortunately he lost the business in the toiletries and gift sector without building it in the perfumery sector. Because there was no one at the company to monitor and support him this problem escalated until the whole Norwegian market was lost. This again emphasises the necessity of choosing the right distributor and then working closely with him. The company now has a UK-based sales manager with responsibility for the territory.

18

Technology Transfer

Dr Carl James, NJM Ltd

When contemplating technology transfer to or from another country, it is essential to scope the operation fully by answering a number of questions, which deal with the nature of the technology transfer, the market and receiving payment. Then it is possible to market the technology.

In dealing across national boundaries, answering those questions reveals complications in terms of business culture, legal protection and public and private finance.

What is technology transfer?

Technology Transfer is the sale or lease of technological know-how to a third party and covers many activities, from licensing patented technology to joint development of an initial design for joint marketing. These demand different types of organisation and relationship.

All the countries involved have a number of mechanisms to support technology transfer. As does the EU through its Framework V Programme and other activities. These involve information services, awareness raising and public support to industry. Determining which of the mechanisms is of use for the transfer involved is a first step. They include:

- public and non-profit organisations, such as regional development organisations, technology advice centres and chambers of commerce
- private consultants, including patent specialists and technology brokers
- research and technology organisations, often attached to universities or science parks

These bodies can be useful for contacts and support activities. They will have membership lists, databases, and issue newsletters to help identify target firms. Some will also offer support services, such as technology audits, skills transfer and, possibly, financial support. Such bodies can be identified through your embassy, the DTI or European Commission contacts.

What is the market?

Market research is a first step in this as in other product areas. However, customers are much more sceptical about unproven technology than established products. Defining the needs of customers and how to approach them is thus very important.

There is a clear differentiation between large and small firms. Large firms will be used to licensing and otherwise obtaining technology. However, if the technology is at an early stage of development, there is always the chance of rejection through the 'Not invented here' attitude, whereby companies resist further development of ideas not originating in their own laboratories. This may be a greater hurdle across national boundaries.

Small firms usually lack specialist staff in these areas. They need considerable help to venture into technology transfer. The sale has either to be very clear or assistance from public bodies may be necessary.

Alternatively, it is possible to form a trans-national network to provide a continuing relationship and support. These are sometimes supported by the EU. To sustain technology transfer activities to any country, it is very useful to have a partner company in that country, with whom there is a regular relationship.

How and when will payment be received?

Technology transfer is hard to sell. It is sometimes possible to gain public support for the process, or there may be a long delay until payment is received, e.g. on royalties from a product, which has taken some time to finally develop and sell.

Technology transfer is often a long-term process. It is therefore important that the parties involved agree on a technical and business plan for the process. The value for money of each stage of the process is useful as basis for a firm agreement. Exploring possible external, usually public, funding for the process can make the difference to viability.

Legal advice on the nature of agreements is always useful. However, the best guarantee is a full understanding of mutual benefits. This operates as well across national boundaries as within them.

Marketing the technology

In addition to standard methods of marketing, networks have a particularly useful role in technology transfer. They involve links with a firm or organisation in one or more countries, which can provide many of the services and the intelligence that it would otherwise be very costly to obtain. Networks operate on the basis of mutual benefit.

Setting up a new network is more expensive than joining an existing one. It involves more searches and more negotiations. However it may be the only option. Joining an existing network, which does not have a UK member, or lacks a member with the particular services on offer may be easier.

Information on networks can be found from organisations such as TII, the Licensing Executives Society or FEICRO. CORDIS – (http://www.cordis.lu/) the Commission's database – and Relay Centres supported by the Commission will have information on both networks and individual firms.

19

Exporting through Franchising

*Manzoor G. K. Ishani, MA, MASA, FRSA,
Solicitor, Mundays*

International franchising

Like pollution, franchising knows no boundaries. One only has to walk down the high street of many European towns to see retail trading units operating systems which have originated from as far afield as Australia and the USA.

Those involved in the service industry have always felt that 'going international' was the preserve of wholesalers and retailers of products. This is simply not true. Franchising is an ideal method by which service providers can export, witness Dyno-Rod which franchises successfully in the USA.

One does not have to be a franchisor in one's own country to be able to franchise abroad. Indeed, there are a number of UK companies (for example, Jigsaw) who do not franchise in the UK but who have used franchising as a vehicle for exporting their goods/services into foreign markets. For a retailer the alternative of opening retail outlets in a foreign country is daunting.

Legislation and precautions

There is no specific legislation for franchising in any of the Nordic countries and therefore normal commercial and competition law applies, although in Finland franchising enjoys a partial exemption for resale price agreements among franchisees. In all these countries franchising is now a well-recognised method of selling goods and services. Scandinavia has a well-educated population with a high disposable income and a taste for British goods and services. However, a company (franchisor) considering franchising into any of these countries should take some basic precautions and conduct a commercial and legal audit of the country to which it proposes to export its business system. The following are some of the things which should be investigated and, where appropriate, precautions need to be taken.

Intellectual property

Intellectual property, such as trademarks, the trade name, copyright, etc., and their protection must be considered at the earliest possible stages and certainly before any deal is done or even serious negotiations begun with a prospective foreign franchisee.

The kernel of the business system which consists of the franchisor's know-how needs to be protected and this is usually done by means of secrecy agreements to the extent that the know-how is secret.

Criteria for selection

Criteria for selecting foreign franchisees need to be established early on. The choice of partner in the foreign country is crucial if the enterprise is to succeed. Indeed, this is the most important aspect of the whole process. No matter how thorough a franchisor has been in all other respects, if it fails in making the right choice of partner it is highly likely that the enterprise will fail.

Assessment of capital requirements

So far as is possible, an accurate assessment of the capital requirements of the foreign franchisee needs to be made and this in itself will help to determine the criteria for selecting a foreign franchisee.

Other precautions

All relevant equipment needs to be evaluated not only as to its availability locally, but also as to technical differences in specification and suitability of that equipment.

It is highly likely that the original scheme or concept will have to be amended if it is to work effectively. It is most important when going international that the franchisor's concept be tested by means of a pilot operation in the foreign country. The pilot (whether run by the foreign franchisee, or the franchisor, or by them jointly) will provide the proving ground for the franchisor's concept, products and/or services and will make an invaluable contribution to ensuring that necessary adjustments are made.

The market

Markets, people, habits, tastes and customs differ from one country to another. All these have to be explored and taken into account; and in a pilot operation, fine tuning can take place to ensure that the transition from what is acceptable in the UK to what is acceptable in the other country is made effectively. The availability or otherwise of premises and rental values vary considerably from one country to another and failure to take such matters into consideration can have serious consequences for a retail operation.

Conclusion

As a method of exporting goods and/or services to far-flung markets, using the capital of others, franchising knows no rivals. It is a method which is particularly well suited for small and medium-sized businesses which do not have the resources necessary to export and who would otherwise, but for franchising, be excluded from exporting to lucrative foreign markets. As Manfred Maus, the Chairman of the European Franchise Federation, said during the Milan Franchising Partnership Fair held in November 1996, 'franchising is the most modern and dynamic form of co-operation for small businesses yet devised'.

20

Electronic Commerce

Clive Smithers, County Durham On Line

WWW and Internet technologies

In the European Union project EUROPAGE, run by County Durham On Line, we have identified different levels of use of the Internet for business, or to put it another way, electronic commerce.

Research

You can use the Internet to support market research, to identify opportunities, to find out more about potential clients and competitors. You will be able to find background materials on countries, economies, sectors, companies, hotels, city maps etc. If you are new to the Web it is well worth getting someone with experience to help you at the start (like your teenage child). If you ask the wrong question, you can be overwhelmed with information. For instance, a search on 'Nordic' will get about 18,500 replies (Japan gets over 1,000,000). If you refine your search by then asking for 'services' within the 18,500 Nordic replies you will get about 160 relevant pages – a much more manageable task.

There is a very good collection of Nordic links at http://www.it-kompetens.com.nordic/, and Aston University has a good set of European links at http://aston.ac.uk/.

Company promotion

Simple Web page

This contains company information and contact details. Of itself it will not generate business – you must market your Web page before it can market for you. With the addition of more pages and a structure to help people move through the information, this becomes the Web site.

Web site

Typically this might include basic company information and contact details; description of main products; location maps; and possibly an on-line (e-mail) information request form. If you have a significant level of export business with specific other companies, you may want to make some or all of this information available in other relevant languages.

On-line catalogues

These can be held on a database on a Web site. It is possible to have different views for different customers – for example, a major high volume customer may have a private view of the catalogue with special prices which only they can use.

Provision of a product or service

Some products or services may actually be provided or delivered using Internet technology. This is particularly true of knowledge- or information-based businesses. With the advent of digital cash it will be possible for customers to pay for each page of information as they download it.

On-line ordering and payment

Using the Internet to take orders from anywhere in the world, and to take and process payment. Secure transaction technology will soon be widely available, and other methods of payment exist for orders taken via the Internet, e.g. corporate purchasing cards or traditional invoicing.

Case Study I
Weircliffe International Ltd

Andy Smith is the Sales Manager of magnetic media degausser and bulk tape erasing equipment manufacturer Weircliff International Plc of Exeter. Their equipment has been used by the video industry to erase previously-recorded magnetic tapes for many years. They have exported for many years, but the growth of the security industry and its use of CCTV has opened a new market for their products.

They have normally sold via local distributors. These were often found at trade shows, where they would be approached by potential distributors. Most of these could be weeded out very quickly, but there were usually one or two who had potential. They also kept an eye out for distributors with a good portfolio of complementary equipment who might take on their products.

They have a standard sterling price list for the whole of Europe (VAT payable at local rates). The prices include freight which is normally by road. For markets such as Scandinavia where air freight is used there is a supplement. In the past they have had to have different models for different markets. However, the standardisation of European voltages at 230V has enabled them to produce Europe-wide models. In addition, the coming of EMU means that they will move to a standard Euro-based price list and the standardisation of UK and European discount rates for distributors. They have started using a Web site (http://www.weircliffe.co.uk/) to market their products. This is possible because the user does not need a demonstration or particular technical knowledge. Purchasers will often pay by credit card.

The Web site includes details of their national distributors so that a potential customer can discuss the product in their own language. One problem has been trapping details of visitors to the site as they are often reluctant to leave their details.

21

The Scandinavian and Nordic Retail Scene

Robert Clark, Corporate Intelligence on Retailing

Denmark

The Danish retail market is the second largest in Scandinavia after Sweden, with estimated sales in 1997 equivalent to ecu28.36 billion. In terms of retail sales per head, Denmark is one of the most affluent markets in Europe – an estimated ecu5,401 and higher than anywhere apart from Switzerland and Luxembourg. The high cost of living (and taxes) in Denmark will obviously offset this, but Danish consumers still enjoy considerable prosperity and the retail trade has benefited from this for many years. The recession of the mid-1990s has not brought about in Denmark the round of mergers that have characterised retailing is so many other European countries, although competition is more intense now than during the 1980s. FDB and Dansk Supermarked are the strongest groups in food and daily goods, while the non-food sector contains well-established buying groups that appear to have resisted the incursion of foreign multiples.

Denmark has a relatively mature retail market, but it has none-theless continued to experience real growth throughout the 1990s almost regardless of downturns in the economy as a whole. Further modest growth is expected in the years ahead; retail sales in 1998 are expected to be about 50 per cent higher than at the start of the decade, while retail price inflation has averaged only about 2.5 per cent a year over the period. Some 75 per cent of retail businesses remain in the ownership of a sole proprietor, with only about 15 per cent in corporate ownership. The proportion of retail sales accounted for by food retailing remains relatively high because many 'daily goods' retail operations would be classified to non-foods retail sectors in other countries.

The largest retail groups in Denmark are:

FDB Co-op	Food and non-food co-operative
Dansk Supermarked	Food and some non-food retailing (owns Netto)
Dagrofa	Food buying group
Ditas	DIY and hardware buying group
Magasin du Nord	Department stores
Aldi Marked	Discount food (owned by Aldi Germany)
Centralkob	Food buying group
Samkob	Food buying group

Finland

The Finnish retail market is of similar size to that of Norway and in 1997 was provisionally worth the equivalent of ecu21.60 billion. This translates as ecu4,221 per inhabitant, which is lower than Norway and Denmark but still considerably higher than Sweden. As in other Scandinavian countries, there are relatively few shops and the retail trade in general is very highly concentrated. There was a major re-structuring in the food and daily goods sector in 1996, leaving Kesko as the dominant group and SOK and Tuko also in stronger positions than previously. Foreign retailers have never played much of a part in Finnish retailing, although the entry of Hennes & Mauritz (Sweden) in 1998 should shake up the clothing sector. Similarly, few Finnish retailers have moved abroad, with the main exception being Stockmann and its interests in Estonia and Russia. As in Sweden and Norway, the distribution of alcohol is through a state monopoly (the appropriately named Alko) and this situation will eventually change under the influence of the EU.

The recession in Finnish retailing finally ended in 1996 and real growth was shown in 1997, with further advances expected for

1998. The recently re-structured major groups are, therefore, now in a good position to benefit from the upturn. Retail sales actually fell in 1992 and 1993 in value terms and did not return to their 1991 level until 1997, so the downturn was much the deepest and longest lasting in Europe – a factor which took a major toll of retailer and consumer morale.

The leading retail groups in Finland are:

Kesko	Food and non-food retailer-owned network
SOK Corporation	Food and non-food co-operative
Tuko	Food and non-food voluntary chain
Alko	State alcohol retailing monopoly
Stockmann	Department stores and non-food specialist retail group

Iceland

(Information provided by the DTI)

The population of Iceland is 270,000 people, with 97,000 households. This sounds small but their purchasing power is high; imports in 1995 were £104 million, the highest per capita excluding Ireland.

Food is sold at the retail level in about 1,200 shops, ranging from hypermarkets to corner shops. The trend is towards bigger outlets. The 24 biggest shops hold 50 per cent of the market. The wholesale/retail food market is dominated by three groupings (Hagkaup, Bónus, Nóatún) accounting for 50 per cent of business. Business is increasingly done by direct contact between retail group and suppliers.

The main three food retailers are:

HAGKAUP	28 per cent of the market, nine retail outlets
BÓNUS	12 per cent of the market, seven retail outlets
NÓATÚN	8 per cent of the market, eight retail outlets

Hagkaup have introduced food shopping on the Internet, Netkaup. This innovation has proven to be successful.

Norway

Norway is the smallest Scandinavian retail market in total sales, these being worth the equivalent of ecu22.91 billion in 1997. In terms of sales per inhabitant, however, the Norwegian figure of ecu5,243 in 1997 is higher than either Sweden or Finland. The retail trade is highly concentrated and the country has under 34,000 retail outlets. They serve one of Europe's most affluent markets and the economy does not appear to have suffered from remaining outside the EU. Similarly, high taxes do not prevent Norwegian consumers enjoying a high standard of living and being accustomed to quality products in clothing, household and electrical goods.

Being on the northern edge of Europe, however, has meant that Norway's retailing has attracted relatively little interest from groups based in other countries and no Norwegian retailer has penetrated very far outside Scandinavia. There are, however, several Swedish and an increasing number of Danish operations in the market and, in a reverse flow, the Norwegian food discounters Hakon and Reitan have been moving into Sweden and Finland. Hakon's strong growth in the 1990s has now given it second position in the domestic market, putting pressure on the NKL Co-op, which itself has formed an interesting alliance with the other Nordic co-ops in 1997. This is essentially to combat the inroads made by IKEA into the co-ops' furniture sales.

The leading retail groups in Norway are:

Norges Gruppen	Food and daily goods voluntary chain
Hakon Gruppen	Food retailer and wholesaler
NKL	Food and non-food retailing co-operative organisation
Reitan	Discount food retailer
Vinmonopolet	State owned alcohol retailer
Norgros	DIY and building supplies buying group
Steen & Strom	Department store retailer

Sweden

The Swedish retail market is the largest in Scandinavia and provisionally worth the equivalent of ecu29.06 billion in 1997. In terms of sales per head, however, Swedish shoppers are spending less than their neighbours – ecu3,289 compared with ecu5,401 in Denmark, ecu5,243 in Norway and ecu4,221 in Finland. Recession and depressed consumer confidence has badly affected retail sales in Sweden, even if this is still one of the most affluent countries in Europe. The retail trade is highly concentrated in terms of ownership, though the country's large size and widespread small town-based population gives a shop density (one per 167 inhabitants) comparable with France. One of the most important events for the trade in 1998 will be the Swedish Parliament's report on the concentration in the food and daily goods sector, dominated by ICA, KF Konsum, D-Gruppen and Axel Johnson.

Being the largest market in the region, Sweden has exported many of its non-food specialists into the neighbouring countries. It is also home to two major pan-European retailers – IKEA and Hennes & Mauritz, although the former actually runs most of its international operations from Denmark and the Netherlands. In the reverse direction, however, the high costs and recent recessionary conditions of the Swedish market have traditionally deterred most foreign retailers from entry. There are signs that this is now changing, with recent examples being the entry of Norway's Reitan (discount food) and the takeover of Ellos mail order by La Redoute (France). One area where change was expected but now appears delayed is in the state monopoly distribution of alcohol (through the Systembolaget), which the EU has in 1997 permitted to continue despite its clear breach of the principles of consumer choice and 'no barriers to trade'.

Sweden's largest retail groups are:

ICA Group	Food (and non-food) retailer buying etc. group
KF Konsum	Food and non-food co-operative
D-Gruppen	Daily goods purchasing group
Systembolaget	State-owned alcohol chain
Axel Johnson	Daily goods and mixed goods etc. retailer and wholesaler
IKEA	International furniture/household goods superstores
Hennes & Mauritz	International clothing retailer

22

Advertising in Scandinavia

Finn Kern, Director, Danish Association of Advertising Agencies (DRB)

The Nordic countries represent an interesting market with a lot of similarities between the countries and a few important differences. The countries, in alphabetical order, are Denmark, Finland, Iceland, Norway and Sweden, to which you may add Faroe Islands and the Aland Islands.

The Nordic countries have a population of 23,575,300 compared to EU's 372,653,600. But in 1996 the GDP per capita in the Nordic countries was $28,220 compared to $19,678 in the EU.

The Nordic countries, the EU and co-operation

Denmark has been a member of the EU since 1973. Finland and Sweden decided to join in 1995 while Norway decided to stay out. However, it is important to note that the Nordic countries have a tradition for a close co-operation which is considerably longer than EU's. More than 30 years ago a common labour market in the Nordic countries was made a reality as well as a passport union between these countries.

The reason why the Nordic countries co-operate so well is that they have a very similar understanding of cultural norms and social values. Although history shows bloody battles between, especially, Denmark and Sweden there has been a closer and closer co-operation between the countries during the last 150 years.

In Denmark, Norway and Sweden the basis of the language is the same, and it is rather easy for the inhabitants of the three countries to understand each other's language in writing but not always when spoken. The Finnish language remains a mystery. Still all the countries are able to share more or less the same cultural norms and social values.

Media situation

It is typical for the Nordic countries that the coverage of daily newspapers is heavy and that reading is intense. The number of newspapers per 1,000 inhabitants is among the highest in the world. Norway is leading with 610 copies per 1,000 inhabitants. The leading quality newspapers (measured by circulation) are the Danish *Jyllands-Posten* (175,687), the Finnish *Helsingin Sanomat* (472,000), the Iceland *Morgunbladid* (53,213), the Norwegian *Aftonposten* (280,000) and the Swedish *Dagens Nyheter* (358,000). Compared with other European countries the Nordic daily newspapers are presenting a considerable number of four-colour advertisements of excellent quality.

Television plays an increasing role. With Finland as an exception, the Nordic countries did not start TV advertising until the beginning of the 1980s. Now the penetration of cable and satellite is quite high, with 66 per cent in Denmark, 36 per cent in Finland, 26 per cent in Iceland, 59 per cent in Norway and 61 per cent in Sweden.

While the legislation about TV advertising is rather similar in the Nordic countries, following the EU Television Directive, there is one important difference between the Nordic countries and Great Britain. Advertising of beer and over-the-counter medicines is not allowed in the Nordic countries and some channels broadcasting via satellite via Great Britain take advantage of this as the advertisers claim that the rules of the broadcasting country should be followed.

The advertising agencies

Even though there are many historical and cultural ties between the Nordic countries, there are also a number of differences which must be taken into account when planning campaigns that take place in more than one country. This is also one of the important reasons why the large internationally owned advertising agencies have established themselves in all or most of the Nordic countries. Also, advertising agencies which are not internationally owned have established a number of agreements for co-operation. Therefore, all advertisers who wish to make campaigns in Nordic countries can either choose an international advertising agency or a chain based on local agencies. Lead agencies will typically be situated in Copenhagen, Denmark or Stockholm, Sweden.

Information about the agencies in the countries in question can be obtained from:

Danske Reklamebureauers Brancheforening (DRB)
Badstuestraede 20
PO Box 74
1003 Copenhagen K
Denmark
Tel: +45 33 13 44 44
Fax: +45 33 11 63 03

Mainostoimistojen Liitto r.y. (MTL)
Vuorikatu 22A 3
00100 Helsinki
Finland
Tel: +358 9 625 300
Fax: +358 9 625 305

Samband Íslenskra Auglýsingastofa (SÍA)
Háteigsveji 3
105 Reykjavik
Iceland
Tel: +354 562 95 88
Fax: +354 562 95 85

Reklamebyraforeningen (NAAA)
Hegdehaugssveien 24
Postboks 2373 Solli
10201 Oslo
Norway
Phone: +47 23 19 60 40
Fax: +47 23 19 60 49

Sveriges Reklamförbund (SRF)
Norrlandsgatan 24
PO Box 1420
111 84 Stockholm
Sweden
Tel: +46 8 679 08 00
Fax: +46 8 679 08 01

23

Direct Mail

Gerry O'Brien

Scandinavia is in some ways like a distant extension of the domestic market. This is particularly true when using direct mail, both for advertising and as a delivery medium. Unfortunately the postage rate to the EU is no longer the same as the UK for basic letters. However, the rates are still competitive, as are those of the various courier companies.

The rules of direct mail marketing are the same as you would use in the UK.

Tandem mailing

If you can identify people and their concerns and you have the budget to do it, you could mail all the decision-makers, sending each a unique letter answering their likely questions. A common leaflet or brochure would usually be adequate, although you may wish to send a more technical leaflet to an IT manager, for instance.

This is a very powerful approach which has worked well for some mailers. It is, of course, expensive and is more appropriate when selling higher priced products.

Identifying the key-decision maker

If you cannot afford to mail more than one person in the same company, you will have to find a way of identifying the key person in the decision-making unit and delivering the most powerful message that you can.

The key person will not necessarily be the final decision-maker – it could be the person most likely to drive the decision, an IT manager for example, who may recognise that a new system is needed. If you can identify that person by phone – and remember that most Scandinavians will be able to speak English – you can then provide them by mail with the product information that they need to influence the decision.

This approach can ensure that your mailings have a very powerful impact. Clearly it can only work if you gather and organise the necessary information – and this is where a customer database will prove its worth.

The customer database

If you are entering a new market it is probable that you will not have a large collection of potential customers. Commercial organisations such as Dun and Bradstreet can provide you with segmented customer information – at a price. It is better to start by talking to your local embassy, the DTI or your local Business Link. Also if you belong to a trade association they may be able to help. You might still have to go to a commercial company in the end – but even if you do, one of these organisations may be able to point you at the right one.

You can store your data on a PC using a standard database product such as Microsoft Access or you can purchase a specialised contact manager such as Maximizer. A contact manager is designed, as its name implies, to keep details of all your contacts and will normally have a WP package and a phone dialler – which works via your modem. It can also hold all your sales contacts and generate mail-merged sales letters. Details of letters sent will be kept for each contact.

Using the database

You may have to phone around to identify decision-makers (and remember you can make large savings using a 'call back' service such as Swiftcall), but once you have done so you can use a postal research questionnaire to get information about your potential customers – domestic or commercial – and you will get the responses in a structured and useful format.

Or you can by-pass the questionnaire and go in cold with a sales pitch. You will have to decide on the best method. Again advice from your embassy or the export promoter (see Sources of Information and Support) is well worth getting and can save you a lot of time.

Delivery

Once you have your sale you have to deliver the goods. Again mail – or a courier company – are an ideal method for low to medium weight articles, especially if they have a comparatively high value. There are normally no restrictions on mail to EU or EEA countries. The main exceptions are associated with dangerous substances. If you are in any doubt the Royal Mail or your courier company will advise you (it is unlikely that the regulations will differ from domestic ones).

If the delivery is time critical you will normally be able to arrange guaranteed delivery times. Again your carrier will advise you.

So, in summary, direct mail is an effective delivery system both for your marketing message and the actual product.

(Information provided by a number of sources including Royal Mail and DHL.)

Part 5

Sales Procedures

24

Intellectual Property

Nigel Swycher, Slaughter and May

Introduction

There is no business today which does not depend for its daily operation upon the use of intellectual property rights (IPRs). Those businesses which create and market new products rely on IPRs to protect their investment in R&D and in their marketing by giving them the security of knowing that the extent to which competitors may copy them and take advantage of that investment is protected by IPRs such as patent rights, design rights and trade mark rights. In addition, confidential information relating to commercial and financial activity, new product development, personnel performance and much else besides is kept secure by the IPR regime for the protection of trade secrets and obligations of confidentiality.

As a consequence of high profile and well-publicised legal disputes between market rivals and the need to retain control over one's operations in an era of increased international trade, businesses today have become far more conscious of the need to address IPRs at all levels. For example, it is now commonplace for companies to seek to register their logos, trade names and the names of their branded products as trade marks. There are, however, many examples of 'blind spots' in corporate IPR policy. For example, many companies which do file for protection of their logos as trade marks tend to overlook the fact that logos are also protectable by copyright law and thus fail to take assignment of that copyright from the independent design agencies which create their corporate or product image.

Registered rights

IPRs may be divided into two categories: those which are registered and those which are not. Registered rights include patents for inventions, trade marks for logos, devices, labels and product packaging, designs for patterns and for industrially manufactured goods which appeal to the eye, as well as plant variety right protection. Unregistered rights include copyright in all types of literary, musical and artistic works – including computer programs – as well as trade secrets and the right of one trader to prevent another trader passing itself off as being connected with him. It is a popular fallacy that a work must be registered or 'copyrighted', since all types of copyright work enjoy automatic legal protection against copying.

Patents

Patents are granted for inventions which are:

- new;
- non-obvious;
- capable of being made or used in any area of industry, including agriculture; and
- not prohibited from being patented on one of a number of public policy grounds.

The maximum duration of a patent is twenty years from the date of first application (an application usually proceeds to grant between 30 and 42 months from that date). Some patents in the pharmaceutical and agrochemical fields may be extended beyond the twenty-year period as compensation for the length of time taken to test them and pass them for use.

Trade marks

Trade marks are signs (words, logos, devices, slogans and so on) which serve to distinguish the activities of one business from those of others. Once registered, a trade mark is potentially eternal, although it must be renewed at ten-year intervals.

Designs

Designs which embody features of pattern, shape, configuration or form that are industrially multiplied by a manufacturer, and which have eye appeal, may be registered at the Designs Registry (which, like the Trade Marks Registry, is part of the Patent Office). Upon renewal, a design registration may be registered for up to five consecutive five-year periods.

Unregistered rights

The main category of unregistered IPR is copyright. There are two types of work protected under copyright law, corresponding to the author's message (literary, musical, dramatic and artistic works) and to the medium by which that message is conveyed (e.g. sound recordings, broadcasts, cable transmissions, editions of published works). Films occupy a middle ground between these two categories, since the director is treated for most purposes as though he is an author even though a film, like a sound recording, is also a vehicle by which an author's work is conveyed to the viewing public. Closely similar to copyright, and also unregistered, is the right which a performer enjoys in his performances. There are also unregistered design rights, rights in trade secrets and confidential information, as well as the right to object to a 'passing off'.

Since the rights just mentioned are unregistered, there is no register from which details of creatorship or ownership can be obtained. This means that a prospective licensee of such a right will frequently have difficulty in identifying the party from whom permission to use it (in the case of copyright, 'clearance') may be sought. Additionally, where such a right is the subject of litigation, the right to own or control it is more likely to be put in issue.

International protection

All of the UK's major trading partners, and nearly all of its minor ones, possess laws which protect IPRs in a way which, if not identical to the UK, is recognisably similar to it on most points of principle. Within the European Union a twofold programme of creating pan-European IPRs and for harmonising the laws of member states on IPR protection means that businessmen have come to expect that, within the Single Market, a uniform standard of IPR protection will apply. This uniformity does not yet extend to the enforcement of IPRs, which means that, where an IPR is infringed in more than one country, 'forum shopping' takes place before the owner of the IPR selects the country in whose courts he seeks to sue.

Maintaining an intellectual property portfolio

Like any other asset, an intellectual property right is only of benefit to its owner if that owner is aware of its existence and extent. Many businesses, however, find it difficult to identify both those rights which they have created and those rights which they use under licence or by virtue of an assignment or other transfer. The burden of record keeping need not be onerous, although it may be exacerbated by factors such as the decentralisation of operations or of record keeping, the frequent restructuring of groups of companies between which IPR are held and the division of records between legal, commercial and personnel departments.

The author wishes to acknowledge the assistance of Dr Jeremy Phillips, Intellectual Property Consultant, Slaughter and May, in preparing this chapter.

25

Trade Mark Protection under the Madrid Protocol

Christopher Cook, Forrester Ketley & Co.

Exporters to Scandinavia may be interested to learn that there is a Trade Mark system known as the Madrid Protocol which covers, *inter alia*, the United Kingdom, Sweden, Denmark, Finland, Iceland and Norway. Under this system, a party can apply for a Trade Mark in the United Kingdom and then, on the basis of the so-called 'home' Application, apply to extend territorial protection to the separate Scandinavian countries.

The advantages of applying for a so-called International Registration under the Madrid Protocol are that there are cost savings to be made over filing six national Applications and since an International Registration is of a unitary nature, any changes by way of assignment, etc. can be recorded centrally with the World Intellectual Property Organisation in Geneva.

In addition, either at the time of filing or subsequently, exporters can designate other territories which are party to the Madrid Protocol. In May 1998 the territories are: Benelux (Belgium, the Netherlands and Luxembourg), China, Cuba, Czech Republic, Germany, Denmark, Finland, France, Hungary, Iceland, Korea (Democratic People's Republic), Lithuania, Liechtenstein, Monaco, Moldova, Norway, Poland, Portugal, Russian Federation, Slovakia, Slovenia, Spain, Sweden, Switzerland and Yugoslavia.

There are, however, what may be perceived as potential disadvantages to filing through the Madrid Protocol system, the first of which is that the International Registration is dependent on the 'home' Application for the first five years. Secondly, the territories for which protection is requested have an eighteen month period in which to deny protection in that territory.

If, at any time, an International Registration is cancelled, then the Trade Mark proprietor can apply to transform the International Registration into national Applications.

Further information can be obtained from your Trade Mark Attorney.

26

Financial Aspects of Exporting to Scandinavia

Kevin Thorne and David White, Grant Thornton

How do financial considerations impact commercial decisions?

Scandinavia presents significant opportunities for UK companies through both its location and its cultural similarities. This is supported by a healthy trading relationship and the fact that Sweden, Denmark and Finland are within the EU and that Norway and Iceland are members of EFTA and the European Economic Area.

Scandinavia accounts for in excess of £6 billion of UK exports, although trade is principally with Sweden and Denmark. Both of these countries offer incentives for inward investment: Sweden through the Invest in Sweden Agency and Denmark through various government packages including grants and subsidised loans. These factors provide a substantial basis for further growth, although this must be supported by adequate financial planning.

Will you be subject to local taxes?

A key question for a UK company exporting to Scandinavia for the first time will be whether its activities give rise to a tax liability outside the UK. If a UK company merely exports to Scandinavia without using local staff it should not be exposed to local tax as it will be trading *with* another country as opposed to trading *within* that other country.

If a UK company does need to create a local presence, it may operate either through a branch of the UK company or through a locally incorporated subsidiary company. The main advantages of a branch operation are that set-up costs may be lower and tax relief can be taken in the UK for any initial trading losses.

The principal advantage of a local subsidiary over a branch is that it may have greater commercial credibility. It is common for UK companies to test the waters with a branch structure which is then converted to a local subsidiary at a later date when operations have become firmly established. This can generally be achieved without significant tax cost.

In preference where should tax liabilities lie?

Following the November 1997 Budget the UK has become a virtual tax haven; small companies will be paying corporation tax at 20 per cent and large companies at 30 per cent for 1999/2000. Accordingly, in most cases it will be preferable for tax liabilities to be incurred in the UK. Indeed, as demonstrated by the headline rates of corporation tax shown in Table 26.1 there is no exception to this rule for small companies exporting to Scandinavia.

Table 26.1 *Corporation tax headline rates*

Country	Federal rate	Local rate	Effective rate
Denmark	34%	–	34%
Finland	28%	–	28%
Iceland	33%	–	33%
Norway	20.75%	7.25%	28%
Sweden	28%	–	28%

If a local subsidiary is registered, dividends may be paid back to the UK from Denmark, Finland and Sweden without withholding tax, provided the qualifying conditions are satisfied. Dividends from wholly owned subsidiaries in Iceland and Norway will suffer a 5 per cent withholding tax.

Generally, profits can be remitted to the UK by branches without a further taxation cost, although professional advice should always be obtained.

What about indirect taxes?

If the customer is in the EU and not in business, e.g. individuals, then UK VAT is chargeable at the applicable rate. However, exports to Scandinavian businesses may be treated as zero-rated in the country of export, although there are additional VAT implications for UK companies exporting within the EU. Additionally, all exports to non-EU countries, such as Norway and Iceland, may be subject to local tariffs and duties depending on the nature of the transactions involved.

Exporting to EU countries

For exports to EU countries it is necessary to prove that the customer is in business, and it is usually simplest to ensure that the customer is VAT registered.

For all intra-EU dispatches an EU sales list must be completed and submitted for each quarter. If the total of exports in any one calendar year exceed the Intrastat threshold (currently £225,000) then there is a requirement to complete monthly Intrastat Supplementary Declarations.

Conclusion

Scandinavia represents a growing market for UK exports and provides many positive attributes for a new exporter, which will increase further with the introduction of the single market. However the financial structure to facilitate exports must be considered together with careful attention to Scandinavia's demands for high standards of quality and punctuality.

27

Providing Exporters with a Business Alternative to Litigation

Karl Mackie, Chief Executive,
Centre for Dispute Resolution (CEDR)

History

In 1989 a group of lawyers got together and decided it was time UK and European managers were afforded a choice when it came to legal disputes. They formed a non-profit making organisation called the Centre for Dispute Resolution (CEDR) which had as its mission the education and promotion of alternative dispute resolution (ADR), a discipline that was becoming increasingly utilised by the commercial worlds of the USA and Australia.

At first we were told that ADR would not work here, that it was not relevant to the English or European legal systems. There was also some concern it would take bread from the mouths of the professionals. It was seen as 'privatised' justice and, as such, would undermine the public justice system, and lead to compromise rather than 'justice' for one particular party. The development of mediation has been driven by pragmatic commercial interests which are more appropriate to modern business practices. It has scope to consider aspects of fairness or realism that a court could not take into account and it places a premium on restoring consensus and relationships, rather than the combative route of litigation.

Today that scope has been recognised. CEDR experienced an exponential increase in its first seven years in the mediations being referred to it, hardly surprising when the average cost savings in professional fees alone was reported in 1997 to be over £250,000 per case (calculated over 40 mediations).

CEDR in Scandinavia

CEDR has trained mediators and users in a number of countries including Denmark, Finland and Norway.

CEDR has also designed/supported ADR schemes for industry in a number of sectors including: banking, construction, telecommunications, IT and transport. Another part of its work has been to encourage companies to include ADR clauses in their procurement contracts so that ADR will always be a first consideration should a dispute arise. One such scheme has been signed up with a major international fast food chain to ensure its franchisees have access to mediation through CEDR should their revenue be affected by another franchisee opening close by.

Importantly for exporters, mediation, the principal procedure in the ADR toolkit, is not bounded by foreign jurisdictions. Neither is it bounded by legal procedures, legal rules or legal remedies. Rarely does a dispute not carry any baggage – historical, current and future agendas of both parties; personal career pressures; competence of managers; customer expectations, etc. These are not legal issues and because of its very legal boundaries, litigation can immediately restrain a 'fair' outcome.

All too often today the temptation for busy managers is to protect themselves by passing the dispute over to the lawyers mainly, I believe, through lack of awareness of any other possible route. The reality is that by doing this they are unlikely to extricate themselves entirely from the dispute and with complex cross-border cases taking anything from five to 25 years, could end up spending far more time than they had ever anticipated.

Another factor to bear in mind is that 94 per cent of cases settle out of court through compromise negotiations by the lawyers as the reality of the risks of an imposed public judgement looms.

Far better to enter into negotiations at the earliest possible stage of the dispute to try to reach a speedy settlement (**most mediations take only 1–2 days**) which will leave all parties with a sense of achievement, the business relationship and future export contracts intact and significant cost savings. Despite the fact that most negotiations referred to ADR are in total deadlock, CEDR achieves a settlement in around 90 per cent of cases.

CEDR today

Nearly ten years after the launch of CEDR, ADR has the support, through membership of CEDR, of all leading law and accountancy firms and a significant representation of multinational and international companies (including 70 per cent of the FTSE Top 25 companies). At any one time, CEDR has between 30–40 mediations ongoing and nearly a quarter of these have an international factor.

This figure is very likely to rise dramatically over the next few years as ADR is increasingly and actively supported by the courts themselves. Lord Bingham, the highest law lord in England, is Chairman of CEDR's Advisory Council and a staunch advocate of ADR. The Commercial Court in London has made over 90 orders to parties to consider an alternative way of negotiating a settlement before coming back to Court. Mr Justice Tuckey, head of the Commercial Court, recently reported that only five such cases have then been referred back to litigation – the others having been resolved primarily through mediation.

While ADR is not a panacea for every occasion, managers cannot afford to remain ignorant of its existence and potential to provide a very effective, commercial solution to their problem. It is easily triggered by an early telephone call to request intervention by CEDR as a neutral broker of negotiations.

Major categories of ADR

- **Mediation** – to assist disputants to reach a negotiated, legally binding outcome. Of all the ADR techniques, mediation is emerging as the most powerful and widely used.

- **Consensus building** – ideal to help a range of interest groups reach a consensus in environment or public policy conflicts.

- **Mini trial/executive tribunal** – a panel made up of a senior executive, appointed by each disputant, and a distinguished neutral listens to formal presentations by both parties. The panel then retires to negotiate a resolution.

- **Early neutral evaluation** – parties agree to have the case heard by a jointly appointed neutral to give an early judgement of the merits.

- **Med-Arb** – the mediator can become arbitrator should the parties fail to agree.

- **Adjudication** – a neutral is appointed to make quick binding decisions until the end of a contract or until appeals to the court or to an arbitrator are completed.

- **Dispute Resolution Adviser/Board** – a neutral or board to resolve disputes in a long-running contract by using any one of the ADR techniques.

- **Ombudsman** – for maladministration in transactions involving citizen or consumer complaints.

28

Exporting to Scandinavia is Easy

DFDS Transport

Distance is no problem

Scandinavia may be a long way from Britain in most people's minds, but getting your goods there should present no problems.

DFDS Transport's customers can, very broadly, be categorised in two ways: those requiring relatively straightforward transport services, and those with a requirement for more specialised 'logistics' packages. Freight service can be provided for any consignment, from a small package to a 500,000 tonnes a year flow of steel.

Small loads can be carried on what are known as groupage services, regular trucks carrying perhaps dozens of smaller consignments operating rather like a public bus service for freight. Consignments are relayed to a strategic hub point until finally reaching their destination – which can be in the most northerly parts of the region, as the DFDS Transport network reaches literally every inhabited part of Scandinavia. For larger consignments, it may be more cost effective to operate a dedicated vehicle direct to destination.

One unique feature of DFDS Transport is that it aims to control all transport operations itself, with its own resources – many freight forwarders may well sub-contract vital activities such as road transport, and thus lose a degree of control over the transport movement.

DFDS Transport

The company operates over 5,000 trailers and containers and a number of specialised containers for bulk traffic or coils of steel. Larger customers may prefer to sign a long-term contract which makes it possible to provide a complete logistics package including perhaps warehousing, specialised transport equipment and information technology links tailored to the customer's requirements. DFDS Transport will, if required, assemble a team of specialist managers to look after the needs of specific businesses.

In fact, virtually all the top UK exporters to Scandinavia use DFDS Transport's services in some form. Leading Swedish car manufacturers are heavily dependent on DFDS Transport for the delivery of automotive parts from British manufacturers. Parts collected on a Monday are available on the production line in Sweden the following Wednesday.

The Scandinavian distribution market has become much more homogenised in recent years, particularly since Sweden and Finland's accession to the European Union, and this is reflected in DFDS Transport's approach. The removal of the need to customs clear consignments in Sweden and Finland has cut bureaucracy and made transport operations more predictable.

Exporters to the region can look forward to further improvements in freight transport efficiency over the next few years. From summer 1998, DFDS Transport's shipping sister company will take delivery of three new freight ferries for its route between Immingham and Gothenburg. These will operate at a higher speed than their predecessors and, when the entire fleet is in operation by the end of 1998, crossing times will be cut from 34 to 24 hours. Sailings will operate more frequently, allowing delivery times from the UK to many parts of Scandinavia to be cut by up to 24 hours.

Faster delivery times from the UK may also make it possible for hard-pressed British exporters, battling the effects of the strong pound, to become more competitive with their continental rivals. Another innovation due to take place in 1998 is the opening of the fixed link connecting Jutland with the rest of Denmark to road traffic. This is expected drastically to speed up journey times by road within the country and, to some extent, to and from Sweden. Journey times will be further cut when a second link opens between Denmark and southern Sweden early in the next century.

29

Warehousing and Contract Distribution in Scandinavia

Tony Elsom, Managing Director,
Distribution Projects Ltd, and Jussi Jalanka,
Managing Director, EP-Logistics Oy

Advantages of outsourcing

Many companies find it advantageous to outsource their logistics operations to a specialist third-party contractor when venturing into new markets overseas. This is because:

- Normally it will save time learning about the country, its transport and warehousing infrastructure, and its unique legislation relating to the transportation of goods and the operation of warehouses. This, in turn, allows the exporting company to concentrate on its core skills which add value.
- It will avoid being tied into long-term commitments and the outlay of large capital sums to acquire resources and facilities in the country concerned.
- It is often uneconomic and too risky to set up a dedicated distribution network in the early stages of breaking into a new market.

Contract types

There are normally two main types of requirement and these can be categorised into either resources-based or service-based contracts.

Resources-based contracts

These are where the customer knows his resources requirements and merely asks the contractor to provide them. For example, a specific number of vehicles, or accommodation for a specific number of pallets etc. While the quotations for this type of contract are easier to compare, the skills of the contractor, and his knowledge of the customers being served may not be fully exploited, because he has not been asked to provide an input to the methodology. In addition, standard and frequency of service are also more or less controlled by the customer, who tells the contractor how much stock to hold or when the orders are ready for delivery.

Service-based contracts

By the same token, service-based contracts define the level of activity and service required, and then it is up to the potential contractor to decide how best to fulfil that requirement, and what resources to allow for it. Service-based contracts are more difficult to compare, because of the different methods different suppliers are likely to propose. However, differences can be minimised and evaluated if the exporting company defines the requirements in detail, and provides comprehensive information to the contractor. In return, the potential contractor should be prepared to show a detailed analysis of the costs for the contract, and also details of his proposed methodology for achieving the required level of service.

Logistics centres

With regard to potential markets, population is concentrated mainly in the south-west part of Finland, around the Helsinki/Turku/ Tampere triangle, and in the southern part of Sweden, around Stockholm and Gothenburg. Again both Norway and Iceland have very concentrated populations, unlike Denmark where there is a much more even spread.

The main ports for import into Finland are Helsinki or Turku, both in the south, and for transit to Russia the ports of Kotka and Hamina, which are close to the Russian border (about 55 kilometres). It is worth noting that Finland's railway gauge is the same as Russia's.

It is also worth noting that the port of Tallin in Estonia is developing rapidly, and has good passenger and cargo ferry links with Finland, and borders with Latvia and south-western Russia.

There are many international transportation companies in Scandinavia, many having foreign co-operation. Typical sites for distribution centres are:

- between Stockholm and Gothenburg;
- the Helsinki area;
- Hyvinkää (50 kilometres north of Helsinki).

Next-day delivery in both countries can be provided up to the Arctic Circle from these centres (e.g. Rovaniemi in Lapland). If a more northerly logistics centre is required, then Oulu to the north of Finland's west coast would be an appropriate place.

Typical prices

Prices and methods of charging for contract storage in Scandinavia are not too dissimilar to those in the UK but, of course, they do vary with the type and quality of service required, and the location. Typical prices (1998), which have been based on research by EP-Logistics Oy, an independent logistics planning consultancy based in Helsinki, are as follows:

- Storage costs 40FIM–45FIM (£4.50–£5.00) per pallet per month, based on about 2,000 pallets stored, plus receiving, handling and despatch costs of between 20FIM–30FIM (£2.20–£3.30).
- Rent for an 8-metre (26 feet) high warehouse is about 40FIM–50FIM per square metre per month (£5–£6 per square foot per annum) in Helsinki, but away from Helsinki rents can be as low as 20FIM–30FIM per square metre per month.
- The average gross cost of a warehouse worker is about FM150,000 per year (£16,500).

As in the UK, prices for transport and distribution vary according to volume carried, distance moved, and the type of service provided. Typical examples are shown in Table 29.2 and 29.3.

The cost of distribution around city areas is about 200FIM–250FIM per hour (£22–£28).

Table 29.1 *Trunking shared services from Helsinki*

Destination town	Distance (kms)	Cost (FIM/M$^3)$	Cost (£/M^3)
Turku	195	70*	7.77
Tampere	190	40	4.44
Kuopio	395	70	7.77
Oulu	606	96	10.66

*affected by Aland Island traffic

Table 29.2 *Trunking full loads from Helsinki*

Destination town	Distance (kms)	Cost (FIM)	Cost (£)
St Petersburg	435	7,500	833
Moscow	1,120	14,000	1,555

Table 29.3 *Shared distribution services from Helsinki*

Destination town	Cost (FIM/M^3)	Cost (£/M^3)	Average drop size (M^3)
Turku	71*	7.88	2.0
Tampere	101	11.22	1.8
Kuopio	100	11.11	2.4
Oulo	105	11.66	3.2

*affected by Aland Island traffic

Choosing a third-party distributor

By adopting the procedure illustrated in Figure 29.1 (developed by Distribution Projects Ltd, an independent logistics and planning consultancy based in Chester) and evaluating properly structured quotations received from the shortlisted suppliers, a preferred supplier, who can fulfil the requirement and who is also cost effective, should emerge.

Figure 29.1 shows the inter-related steps which should be taken to evaluate and select a supplier. It is essential to follow a structured selection pattern to choose the right contractor at the right price. The procedure illustrated will help to ensure that the operation is well defined, competitive quotes are obtained and that the contractor can do the job.

As part of the process for choosing a supplier, a shortlist of those contractors who are likely to be able to meet the requirements will need to be drawn up. At this stage it is also highly desirable to ensure that the contractor demonstrates a record of financial stability.

Once the shortlist of contractors has been compiled, the five main elements to selection are:

- specification of the operation and compilation of the logistics database which forms the basis of the invitation to tender (ITT) to undertake market testing;
- issue of the ITT to a shortlist of suppliers;
- evaluation of tenders received;
- negotiation of the contract details with the preferred supplier;
- post-contract preparation for implementation and control.

Management of third-party distribution contracts

A letter of intent will need to be issued to the preferred supplier, and for both sides to agree the legal framework and code of practice for operating the contract, together with an implementation schedule. At this juncture, it will be necessary to agree more precisely:

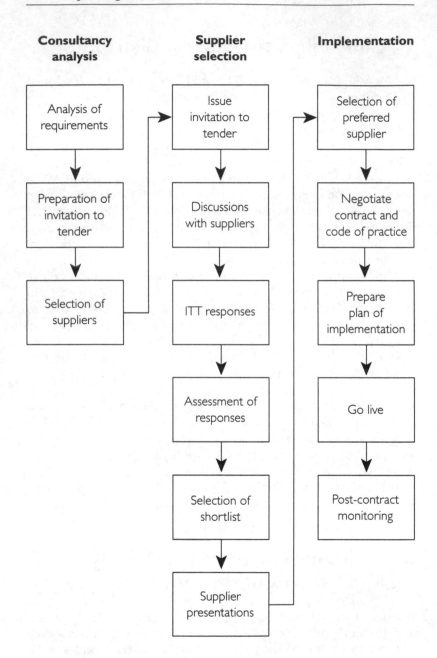

Figure 29.1 *Major contract development*

- service standards and environmental conditions for stock;
- treatment of returns and performance reporting;
- contingency and training requirements costs;
- order and stock-tracking procedures;
- criteria for future price adjustments.

Future changes in requirements which can be identified as far as is possible at the pre-contract stage, and the criteria for adjusting prices, if clearly defined, will help towards maintaining an amicable relationship.

The use of professional advisers

Provided they are independent of any supplier of contract services, the use of specialist advisers can be beneficial in the following ways:

- They will have a knowledge of the distribution industry and will either have databases of information or will know the sources of relevant information.
- They will have developed evaluation and modelling techniques which can be used to help determine the approximate cost of a supply chain before approaching a potential contractor with a 'blank cheque'.
- If experienced, they will have performed in a number of industries and markets, and therefore will have knowledge of 'best practice', which can be passed on to their clients. This means that the potential exporter starts higher up the learning curve.
- New projects are variable in content and will benefit from people who can concentrate on the task and absorb the additional workload, thus enabling operational management to continue to devote time to added-value activities.
- Because advisers have less distraction, they are also more likely to evaluate alternative methods which help the exporter distribute products efficiently.

Part 6

Trade Finance

30

UK Banking Services for Exporters

Martin Morgan, International Business Manager, North West Region, Lloyds Bank Commercial Service

All the banks offer a similar range of international trade services. But the types and varieties of these products differ in the features and benefits on offer. Here is an overview of the main services.

Foreign exchange

The volatile nature of modern international financial markets, where exchange rates can fluctuate rapidly and widely, presents companies with inherent risks. Banks, therefore, have established a range of mechanisms to manage foreign currency risks. There is, however, usually a trade-off between cost and the amount of risk minimisation.

Spot rate

Spot rate is used for currency exchanges that are to take place virtually at once. Delivery of the currency is normally two business days after the deal has been struck.

Forward contract

Forward contract is made between an exporter and a bank for the sale of a specific quantity of currency. The rate is fixed at the time of the contract with delivery of the currency at an agreed future date. The maturity of the contract can either be fixed, i.e. for settlement on a specific date, or option dated, i.e. for settlement on or between two specific dates.

Currency options

These are more complex but flexible instruments. They provide a greater degree of flexibility by giving the holder the right, but not the obligation, to buy or sell an agreed amount of a specified foreign currency at a pre-determined rate of exchange on a future date. Unlike forward contracts, the holder remains free not to use the option if that decision is more advantageous.

When buying currency options, the cost is always certain from the outset as the buyer pays a non-refundable premium for the product. Minimum option amounts are quite large, depending on the bank.

Foreign currency accounts and loans

Deposit and current accounts are available in a wide range of currencies to assist with the management of currency transactions. Cheque books, currency overdrafts and loan facilities are all available. When business is regularly transacted in the same currency a company is able to utilise currency from payments received against payments made, thus avoiding the exchange rate risk.

More sophisticated and specialist foreign exchange 'hedging' mechanisms, such as currency swaps, are available through the banks' treasury departments.

Methods of payment

Trading overseas opens wide opportunities and sets unusual challenges. Selling abroad adds an extra dimension to the risks and rewards of doing business. How can exporters be assured of getting paid? Banks offer a variety of services to simplify and assist the payments process. These are listed in order of preference from the exporter's point of view.

Advance payment

Although the most secure method, from an exporter's point of view, its use is relatively rare in ordinary goods/services trade, being more common for large capital items.

Documentary letter of credit

This is the next most secure method of payment. A documentary credit is a written undertaking given by a bank on behalf of the buyer to pay the seller an amount of money within a specific time, provided the seller presents documents strictly in accordance with the terms laid down in the letter of credit. From an exporter's point of view this substitutes bank risk for buyer risk.

The banks deal in the documents and not in the goods/services to which they refer, and therefore it is vital that the company complies with the terms laid down in the letter of credit. Letters of credit can be complicated and it is important to get bank advice at an early stage.

Bills for collection

With this method, the documentation is handed to the exporter's bank, which sends them to the importer's bank. The bank receiving the collection notifies the buyer that it has received the documents and the terms on which they will be released.

Open account

Open account is the least secure form of payment. However most of the UK's trade with western Europe and North America is conducted on an open account basis, the most simple, straight-forward and flexible method available. Payment is obtained by sending relevant documents to the buyer for immediate payment or for payment at a specified time. While the buyer may pay by cheque, the supplier will have to pay bank collection charges and the risk of delay and non-payment exists. To avoid these disadvantages, it is preferable for the buyer to arrange payment by SWIFT or telegraphic transfer.

Credit insurance

In an unpredictable trading environment, there is a risk to the seller from the uncertainty of payment from the buyer. There are additional political and country risks for exporting companies.

Credit insurance can mitigate against a wide variety of these risks including commercial risks – insolvency of the buyer, failure of the buyer to pay the insured within eight months of the due date of payment; and political risks – war, action by a foreign government which prevents performance of the contract, cancellation of import licence, public buyer default.

The level of indemnity differs between insurers, but normally covers up to 90 or 95 per cent of the invoice value.

NCM Credit Insurance Ltd (which took over the short-term credit insurance activities of ECGD in 1992) remains the largest provider in the UK of short-term (up to 180 days) credit insurance for exporters. A number of other institutions such as Trade Indemnity Plc also provide cover. Credit insurance of a medium/long term nature, or which relates to project finance can be obtained through export credits guarantee departments (ECGD).

Bonds, indemnities and guarantees

When companies are involved in larger value contracts, there may often be a requirement to provide security against advance payments, performance of contract, etc. Bonds, indemnities and guarantees can be issued either in banks' standard English Law format or issued through correspondent relationships abroad where local rules prohibit external guarantees.

Short-term finance

International trade can involve larger credit periods as well as delays in payment both on the part of the buyer and, occasionally, the overseas bank. A large proportion of international trade transactions are funded through bank overdrafts (48 per cent according to the Fifth Survey of International Services Provided To United

Kingdom Exporters commissioned by the Institute of Export & NCM Credit Insurance Ltd). However, to help ease cashflow problems the banks offer a range of specialist short- or medium-term finance packages.

Information technology

Electronic delivery of trade and international banking services is becoming increasingly widespread with various systems on offer including trade and payments services, cash management, market information and electronic communication.

Trade promotion services

All the clearing banks offer, to a greater or lesser degree, additional services to assist companies with researching or breaking into new markets. Most are able to provide general advice on specific markets, technical advice and assistance, economic analysis (including interest and exchange rates) and terms of trade. Through their own overseas branches or correspondent banks, most banks can make enquiries abroad, circulate trade literature and obtain introductions to potential trading parties.

31

Export Credits

The ECGD

The ECGD

For many years ECGD has been the UK government body that helps UK exporters by insuring them against the risks of non-payment by overseas buyers. It offers four main services to the UK exporting community which:

- enable exporters to offer finance packages providing credit to buyers, while receiving cash on delivery through the provision of guarantees to banks in the UK;
- enable exporters to offer finance at favourable fixed interest rates;
- give exporters confidence to sell overseas by providing insurance against non-payment on export contracts;
- protect UK companies investing overseas against certain political risks.

ECGD provides support for business in the project, capital goods, construction and services sectors – much of which involves long delivery periods and/or credit requirements, typically between two and ten years.

ECGD guarantees loans from British banks to overseas banks/ companies where credit of two years and more is given to an overseas buyer. The loan enables the buyer to pay cash to the exporter as the goods are delivered. The loans can be arranged especially for one large contract or project or to provide finance for a number of potential contracts – credit lines. The loans can be made available in a range of currencies and, because of ECGD's involvement, will normally enable exporters to offer attractive fixed rates of interest to buyers. Additional protection is available should the exporter need to terminate the contract part way through. Some loan packages can include support for termination settlements/ arbitration awards. The alternative is to take insurance as mentioned later.

Certain conditions attach to ECGD's finance facilities, the most important of which are that they should:

- provide at least two years' credit;
- finance a maximum of 85 per cent of the contract value, with the 15 per cent balance being payable by the buyer to the exporter before the start of the credit period;
- be made by banks who are authorised under the Banking Act 1987 and are acceptable to ECGD.

Insurance

ECGD can also assist exporters for goods sold on a 'cash' basis, providing cover against the main commercial and political risks which arise during the manufacturing and credit periods. Commercial risks are those connected with the buyer, such as insolvency or default; political risks are broadly those outside an individual's control, such as hard currency shortages, civil war or unrest. ECGD is able to pay up to 95 per cent of any such loss incurred.

Insurance is also available for investments made overseas in the form of loans and equity. This insurance covers losses which could result from specific political risk such as an overseas government seizing or confiscating an investment, restrictions on remittances or the outbreak of war or civil war.

Other products offered by ECGD include insurance against unfair calls and calls made as a result of specified political events under bonds or guarantees given in connection with an export contract, and insurance against exchange rate fluctuations where a lender requires a foreign currency price to be quoted.

ECGD charges premium for its services. The rates depend on various considerations, e.g. the country, the nature of the project, its duration and the type of risk to be covered. The charge will therefore vary from case to case. ECGD's underwriters are able to provide indicative rates for any prospective business.

Following the privatisation of ECGD's comprehensive short-term insurance business, cover for consumer goods, raw materials and the like is now provided by the private sector. Exporters of these goods should seek the advice of their broker or private sector export credit agencies. ECGD continues to provide short term insurance for larger sales of capital goods and projects.

This chapter has attempted to provide a brief summary and introduction to ECGD's facilities. It is not, however, intended to be exhaustive, nor does it constitute any commitment to offer cover or support of any type in any particular case. You are advised to consult your own legal or technical advisers as to the full implication of seeking cover or support from ECGD.

32

Grants and Assistance

Gonzalo Shoobridge, NJM Ltd

The European Commission (EC) stresses the need to mobilise all suitable initiatives to boost and exploit SMEs' scope for promoting growth and employment as well as coping with the weaknesses inherent in their smaller scale. To achieve this goal, the EC and the UK government have proposed a number of priority policies and measures designed to enhance the competitiveness and internationalisation of SMEs.

There are a large number of export assistance grants and subsidies available to UK SMEs. In order to obtain external funding, in most of the cases, it is necessary to fill application forms for specific grants. Before you apply to a grant you should bear in mind the following issues:

- It is rare for a grant to finance 100% of the costs of your project, be ready to put up some of your own capital.
- Grants are only available for specific projects, the process of company development does not qualify for grants, the project must not be underway already.
- The project must help achieve the aims of the grant provider.
- You must show that the project would not achieve the same benefits without the grant.
- You will need to prepare a business plan.
- It is worth paying for help to apply for grants worth £ 50,000 or more. Some accountants and consultants are grant experts.

- Make personal contact with an individual involved with administering the scheme in order to get advice on whether it is worth applying and help with completing the application.
- As for application deadlines, they vary for each type of grant. Some of them have fixed deadlines and others have open call for application throughout the year.
- Application forms normally ask for the project description, the benefits the project offers, a detailed work plan and general information about your company.
- The grant provider will want to monitor how the money is used therefore it is essential to keep records of all your expenses and project activities.

All the following are grants, advice and general support for UK SMEs currently exporting or planning to export for the first time.

SMEs – Multiannual Programme (1997–2000). Grants to help SMEs to Europeanise and internationalise their activities. A variety of support measures, financial and advisory, to improve business know-how, facilitate growth and encourage transnational co-operation of SMEs. Sponsored by the EC, but administered through the Government Offices for the Regions. EC, Directorate General (DG) XXIII Brussels Tel: (00) 322 296 5001

EC: Ibex – Trade Shows. Organises pre-arranged meetings between large enterprises and SMEs on an international scale. Supports up to 25% of costs.
DG XXII Fax (00) 322 296 7558
DG XVI Fax (00) 322 296 3273.

ECGD: Foreign Exchange Risks. See the previous article by ECGD.

TEC: Business Support. Provision of a range of services and grant funding schemes to assist business start-up, business expansion and business development (Business planning; export and marketing). Sponsored by the Department of Employment's Training, Enterprise & Education Directorate (DE-TEED).
Tel: (0191) 516 0222 Tel: (0181) 547 3934 Tel: (0171) 377 1866.

LEDU: Business Support. Advisory help and financial assistance to enable new business start-ups succeed. LEDU (Local Enterprise Development Unit) Tel: (01232) 491031.

Queen's Awards: Export Achievement Award for outstanding achievements in exporting goods or services. Sponsored by Her Majesty's Government. Tel: (0171) 222 2277.

CT: Futurestart Community Venture Fund. Covers finance for business start-ups, company expansion, etc. Centreway Development Capital Limited. Tel (01675) 466796.

HM Customs & Excise – Free Zones. Goods may be moved without payment of customs duty and similar import charges, including VAT. Tel (0171) 865 4634.

National Westminster Bank Plc.: Export Excellence Awards for exporting professionalism. Tel. (0171) 920 5486.

British Midland's Export Award Initiative. Tel. (0171) 494 1331.

The Department of Trade and Industry (DTI) offers grants and subsidised support for SMEs intending to export in a large variety of ways: export market research studies and overseas fieldwork, export Information for desk research, enquiries for products or services, location by name and address of a person or firm in an export market recommended by the DTI to represent the exporter in that market either as an agent, distributor, importer or manufacturer under licence, awards on exporting performance, consultancy service to assist companies in identifying, evaluating and enhancing their communication skills in non-English speaking markets, subsidy or Grant for exhibitions or trade fairs held overseas. For more information contact your local Department of Trade and Industry (DTI). *See also Section 3 Accessing the Market – Sources of Information*

33

Protected Export Finance – Competing on Equal Terms with Local Suppliers

Mark Hind, Marketing Director,
Griffin Credit Services Limited

Successful exporting can provide additional profit and stability to a business by broadening and diversifying its customer base. But like most opportunities where the potential rewards are high there is a cost. An export order can be hard to get, payment from an overseas buyer even more so. There are still huge differences between selling to customers in Swansea and those in Stockholm, Stavanger or Savonlinna.

Businesses embarking on the export trail need to prepare thoroughly, get it right first time and, most importantly, compete on equal terms with local suppliers. That means having the cash to fund more sales; profits protected so there are no wasted sales; effective payment collections in the language and currency of your buyers and the ability to trade in the most competitive currencies, while limiting foreign exchange risk.

Protected export finance and profit

A protected export finance service, like those on offer from Griffin, can help a business make exporting a profitable part of their sales strategy. It combines sales-linked finance, bad debt protection, payment collections and transmission services, all the ingredients needed to offer overseas buyers credit terms that are really competitive, even against local sources of supply. And, with the help of the latest leading edge technology, the services can be combined and tailored to meet the exporting needs of individual businesses and individual export markets. An exporter can sell more safely and, with long-range credit control and payment processing taken care of, devote more time and resources to sourcing and selling to new buyers.

For businesses involved in overseas trade, technology plays an essential role in helping the exporter keep in touch with their factoring company. This means they can react quickly to business opportunities, access management information and process credit requests for new and existing buyers more efficiently and quickly. Griffin aims to reply within 48 hours of a credit request. The increased use of technology allows the factoring company to offer a more bespoke level of service; one that is fast and effective and genuinely adds value to the exporter/buyer relationship. Factoring companies who provide technical links with their clients can become integral to the export cycle by connecting into day-to-day systems and procedures; the factor's systems no longer run alongside the exporter's own systems – they become part of them.

Overseas business

This becomes even more apparent when the factor is providing overseas customer collections. Credit control can be difficult at long range. Language, time zones, even cultural differences conspire to make the job harder. Satellite links and electronic datalines now give faster, more efficient communications with an exporter's markets. The advantages start with the initial credit checking process, right through to shorter payment transmission times, as payments are cleared locally and remitted to the UK by SWIFT (an electronic bank-to-bank system). The factor's technology provides exporters with an immediate, up-to-date picture of their sales ledger. The exporter can instantly view activity on their buyers' accounts, wherever they are located.

Griffin is the only UK financial services company to have all its clients linked electronically. The unique Ledgerline PC, provided free of charge as part of the service, gives on-line control and access to instant communications throughout the world. It shares information and powerfully enhances the exporter's own business resource.

The need to communicate quickly and effectively with factoring companies throughout the world is essential in order to attract more businesses exporting overseas. A new system devised by Factors Chain International (FCI), of which Griffin is a member – EDIFACT – provides for the electronic transfer of cross-border invoices which helps minimise some of the barriers to international trade. Seamless EDI solutions link exporters with 45 countries worldwide. Exporters can compete on equal terms with overseas competitors, safe in the knowledge funds will be transferred promptly and payments are guaranteed.

Conclusion

By using protected export finance services an exporter is releasing cash tied up in a very important asset – the sales ledger. The business is not borrowing, just making their assets work harder for them. In turn, this can free other assets to help raise finance for more strategic purposes, rather than meeting day-to-day operating expenses. Overseas buyers may also welcome not having to provide their bank with security in advance, which they would have to do if an exporter insisted on letters of credit – making the exporter truly competitive against local sources of supply.

34

Leasing

Introduction

In the UK there can be considerable tax advantages in using a leasing company to help finance the sale of capital goods. It is not possible to 'export' those benefits. Additionally, UK interest rates have been historically higher than in most of the Nordic countries. Therefore if you are considering using leasing as a way of promoting your goods in Scandinavia it will normally be necessary to use the services of a locally based leasing company.

Mechanics of leasing

The mechanics of leasing in most of the Nordic countries, tax considerations aside, are basically the same as in the UK.

Hire purchase

Sometimes known as asset purchase, this 'non-tax based' form of purchase offers no tax advantages. It is used by both individuals and companies to purchase equipment, especially motor vehicles. This is the only form of asset finance where the asset will eventually be owned by the user.

Finance lease

A 'tax-based' form of lease, in which ownership of the asset never passes to the lessee, although the latter is committed to the full cost of the asset. Normally, the lease will run for the life of the asset (typically two–seven years). At the end of the lease period the lease can either be extended at a greatly reduced amount or the asset can be sold to a third party and the bulk of the resale value returned to the lessee as a rental rebate.

Operating lease

The lease will not run for the full life of the asset and the lessee will not be liable for its full value. The lessor or the original manufacturer or supplier will assume the residual risk. This type of lease will normally only be used when the asset has a known resale value, for instance, aircraft or vehicles. A type of operating lease known as contract hire includes maintenance. As the leasing company may eventually own the asset they are often keen to use contract hire as this will ensure that they have a saleable asset at the end of the day.

There is an international standard, International Accounting Standards No. 17 (IAS17) *Accounting for Leases*, that is widely used in the region as well as in the UK. This governs both finance leases and operating leases. The tax position of leases is broadly similar across the region. While this will not directly affect the exporter it is important that you use a reputable locally based company that does understand these issues.

Denmark

There is no special legislation on leasing, although leasing companies are generally regarded as providers of medium term finance. The Association of Danish Finance Houses introduced a standard lease in 1995 and this is gradually becoming the standard lease document. Rentals are paid either monthly or quarterly and can be in advance or in arrears. Some leasing companies will also combine invoice discounting (for fuller details about invoice discounting see Chapter 33) with a leasing service. Finance and Operating leases are both accounted for in the same manner. Both local legislation and IAS17 are used when accounting for leases.

Finland

Leasing has been available in Finland since the 1960s, mainly from local banks. Only about 6–7 per cent of machinery and equipment sales are financed by leasing, although local finance houses hope that this will rise to about 10 per cent. There is no special legislation on leasing, although finance companies must be registered and are subject to various conditions relating to liquidity, capital adequacy etc. All relevant EU directives have been incorporated into local legislation. Provision is made for the rescheduling of debt in a similar manner to the US 'Chapter 11' protective bankruptcy legislation.

Norway

Leasing was introduced into Norway in 1963 and is mainly supplied by broadly based financial institutions. The Norwegian leasing industry went from boom to (almost) bust in the 1980s as it followed the Norwegian economic cycle. The industry is now more cautious. As in the UK, the memory of this cycle is strong in all sectors of the economy and is likely to make would-be purchasers more realistic in taking on liabilities; additionally there have been tax reforms to reduce the risk of another boom and bust cycle. Consequently it should be possible to attract lease finance for a well thought through sale and lease proposal.

There is no special legislation on leasing. There is a standard lease contract that is widely used. Conventional finance leases are available and widely used. There is also a form of 'discount lease' where the lease company will purchase the leased good from the supplier, but the latter will retain some residual obligation to the lease company in the event of default by the end purchaser. This is probably best avoided by a UK exporter. In 1996 proposals were made by a government committee that smaller companies (about 85 per cent of all lease contracts) could be treated as the legal owner of a leased asset for accounting purposes. This is seen as a positive incentive to use leasing products.

Sweden

Sweden has a large and innovative leasing market with SMEs representing the bulk of lessees. However, large corporates and local authorities also make use of lease facilities. Leasing represents about 50 per cent of all financial credit and about 15–20 per cent of all machinery and equipment is financed by leasing companies. There is no special legislation on leasing although there is general legislation incorporating EU directives that covers finance houses. Legislation on contracting and hiring is applied to finance leases. Individual finance houses have their own standard leases and these will generally specify which legislation will apply to the lease. Lease companies will often seek to pass some residual liability for the performance of equipment to the supplier. Accounting practices are similar to IAS17.

Conclusion

Leasing is a well-proven method of financing sales and the Nordic countries have a strong leasing sector. UK exporters will need to identify a leasing company that is active in the country to which they are exporting and as many lease companies are only based in a single country this means that they might be dealing with a number of different finance houses. It is important that exporters choose a reputable company that understands both their product and the local market. Details of local lease companies can be obtained from the local leasing association (a list can be found at the end of this chapter). If you already deal with a UK based company it is worth finding out if they operate in Scandinavia or have any local affiliates.

Finance leases are probably the most appropriate method of leasing and exporters should check very carefully what residual liabilities they will be left with. Many liabilities can be covered by insurance and exporters should ensure that lease contracts require that the lessee (end purchaser) is responsible for this.

Information for this chapter has been supplied from a number of sources including LEASEUROPE.

Leasing associations

Finnish Finance Houses Association
c/o Finnish Bankers Association
Museokatu 8 A
PO Box 1009
FI-00100 Helsinki
Secretary Mr Juuso Jokela
Tel: +358 9 405 6120
Fax: +358 9 405 61291

Finansieringsselskapenes Forening
(The Association of Norwegian Finance Houses)
Postboks 1310
VIKA N - 0112 Oslo
Managing Director Mr Frank Myhre
Tel: +47 22 01 41 80
Fax: +47 22 01 41 84

Danske Finansieringsselskabers Forening
(Danish Finance Houses)
Dr Tvaegade 16
Box 9005
DK - 1022 Copenhagen K
Tel: +45 33 15 15 32
Fax: +45 33 12 24 24

AFINA – Association of Swedish Finance Houses
Strandvägen 7B, entre 2
Box 14034
S-104 40 Stockholm
Tel: +46 8 660 68 90
Fax: +46 8 662 76 12

Svenska Bankföreningen, Bolagsavdelningen
(Swedish Bankers Association, Finance Company Department)
Regeringsgatan 38
Box 7603
S-103 94 Stockholm
Director Gösta Fischer
Tel: +46 8 453 44 00
Fax: +46 8 453 44 15

Part 7

Support Services

35

Legal Aspects of Exporting into Scandinavia

Martin Börresen, Lagerlöf & Leman

General

The legal systems of the Scandinavian countries, including Finland and Iceland, are civil law systems originating from a common legal tradition based on statutes. Many important acts in the area of commercial law have been prepared by the work of joint committees between all or some of the Scandinavian countries.

Since 1973 Denmark has been a member of the European Community, now the European Union (EU). Sweden and Finland joined the EU on 1 January 1995, and although Norway and Iceland are not members, they are parties to the European Economic Area (EEA) Agreement which means that important principles of EU law, eg on the free movement of goods and competition, also apply in these countries.

The common legal tradition and the joint legislative work of the Scandinavian countries, as well as the recent influence of European law, has meant that in important respects these countries have very similar laws in the commercial field. However, there are also differences which may be significant in specific cases.

Contracts

The basic principle of freedom of contract applies in all Scandinavian countries unless otherwise stated. Except for some specific contracts that must be in writing, such as sales and mortgages of real property, there are no formal requirements for the formation of a contract. Oral agreements are as binding as written, although written contracts are recommended. There is no requirement of a consideration, which generally means that an offer is binding unless otherwise stated in the offer.

The legal business entities in Scandinavia are public and private limited companies, general partnerships and limited partnerships. The limited companies are generally listed in official registers, such as in Sweden at the Patent and Registration Office (PRV), where updated information on the companies can be acquired. Foreign companies may also register a branch having a manager representing the company in the country, or only have a representative office. The latter form of representation does not have to comply with any specific administrative requirements.

Distribution

Since all of the Scandinavian countries are either members of the EU, or parties to the EEA Agreement, goods may generally be exported into these countries without duties, licences or similar requirements, although some specific requirements exist, eg regarding military material and food products.

Of the different forms of distribution, such as distributorship, franchising and commercial agents, only the latter form has been regulated by comprehensive legislation. Thus, there is no specific legislation on distributorship or franchise agreements in Scandinavia, which in principle means that the parties under general contract law can freely agree on the terms and conditions for such contracts.

As regards commercial agents, all Scandinavian countries have enacted legislation adapted to an EC directive on commercial agents, containing mandatory provisions on inter alia commission and indemnity after termination of the contract.

Competition law and product liability

Distributorship agreements and similar arrangements may be incompatible with the competition laws of the Scandinavian countries. All of the Scandinavian countries basically adhere to the principles of EC law prohibiting, inter alia, agreements between undertakings which restrict competition. Restrictive agreements may in some cases be exempted under group exemptions.

As regards non-contractual product liability, the Scandinavian countries have introduced new legislation based on an EC directive, which provides for strict liability for 'security imperfections' causing personal injury and material damage to consumers.

Disputes and legal advice

Clauses on governing law and arbitration are generally to be recommended in international contracts. In Sweden arbitration has a long tradition and is a well established method of resolving commercial disputes. The Arbitration Institute of the Stockholm Chamber of Commerce (SCC) is internationally respected and frequently referred to in international contracts. The proceedings are often conducted in foreign languages and the rulings are enforceable as court judgements.

Denmark is a party to the Brussels convention and all of the other Scandinavian countries are parties to the Lugano convention, which means, for example, that British judgements can be enforced in Scandinavia.

Naturally, exporting into Scandinavia may require professional legal advice. This brief overview of the Scandinavian legal systems cannot substitute legal advice for any specific transactions. Issues of intellectual property law, public procurement, taxation as well as general commercial law may, in any such case, require legal expertise and it should be considered that the laws of the Scandinavian countries may vary in important respects.

For legal advice, contact a member of the national bar organisation. In Denmark, Norway, Sweden and Finland lawyers are called *advokat* (*asianajaja* in Finnish); and in Iceland *lögmadur*. The larger law firms are generally well experienced in advising foreign clients.

36

General Accounting Principles for Nordic Countries

This chapter is intended to give a general overview of accounting and audit requirements in the Nordic countries in so far as they will affect the subsidiaries or local offices of UK companies. Therefore it does not deal with issues related to public and quoted companies. The article looks at the Nordic region as a whole, although there will be differences from country to country. Many of the larger accountancy practices produce more detailed country guides covering accountancy and tax issues and these are normally available free. Contact phone numbers are shown at the end of the chapter.

Audit requirements

Generally accepted accountancy principles (GAAP) are often the basis of local accountancy legislation and practice. Recommendations of the International Accounting Standards Committee are also being adopted, as are the appropriate European Commission directives. The financial year will usually be the calendar year or in some countries a year based on quarter days. In some circumstances a yearend that is the same as a parent company's UK yearend may be permitted.

Independent auditors must be appointed annually, normally at the AGM. Auditors will normally belong to a professional body approved by the government, although in some circumstances a foreign auditor can be given permission to carry out the audit.

In some circumstances there will be no audit requirement for partnerships and sole proprietors with fewer than ten employees. Also branches of companies registered in another EU state, such as the UK, will not normally require auditing as long as the parent is audited in keeping with normal EU practices.

There is usually a time limit within which annual accounts must be audited and filed. However, smaller businesses whose turnover and capital fall below certain thresholds may be exempt from the requirement to file accounts in some countries.

The subsidiary must keep proper financial records in the same manner as is required in the UK. There may be a requirement to keep records in the local language. There is usually a requirement to keep records for a fixed period. Typically, vouchers for six years and accounts for ten years, although this can be as low as five years. Firms that carry out most of their business overseas can sometimes obtain permission to keep their records in their country of origin. Records will typically include items such as: general ledger, accounts receivable and payable, bound ledger containing the annual accounts and auditors' opinion, board and shareholders' meeting minutes and official correspondence between the company and its auditors.

There can be differences between public accountants and registered accountants (sometimes known as approved accountants or accountants registered at the local chamber of commerce), the latter being allowed to audit smaller private companies.

Other factors to take into account

Inventories

Inventories are normally valued at the lower of FIFO or market cost.

Leases

International Accounting Standard 17 is becoming more widely accepted for the treatment of leases. If a UK exporter is using leases as part of his sales effort this will probably not affect him, as the asset will be the responsibility of the leasing company. However, if he is using leasing to acquire assets for his own business it will. This will also apply to vehicle leases. Major leasing companies will normally be able to advise on lease taxation issues.

Goodwill

Goodwill will normally be required to be amortised at approximately 10 per cent a year.

Payroll

When foreign companies establish operations in Finland, Sweden and to a large extent other Nordic countries they find that the extremely high and complex employer's dues necessitate rather involved payroll accounting.

VAT

There is still a jungle of country-specific exemptions and loopholes.

Currency gains and losses

As much of the Nordic area as well as the UK will be outside the Euro Zone for the immediate future, it is possible that foreign subsidiaries will have to account for currency losses or gains. Typically, assets and liabilities denominated in foreign currencies will be valued at the current exchange rate at the yearend and be included in the balance sheet. Unrealised gains and losses will be included in the income statement or similar entity.

Further information

Detailed information guides are available covering individual countries from some of the major accountancy practices including:

Price Waterhouse	0171 939 2117 or 3000
Ernst and Young	0171 928 2000

[Information in this chapter was provided by national accountancy bodies, individual accountancy practices and academics.]

37

Scandinavia – a Marketing Sketch

Robert Rangecroft, Joint Managing Director,
RNP Limited

Some marketing basics

A first question might be what do we mean by Scandinavia? Is it a geographical area or just a cultural idea? It has never been a political entity and the numbers alone should make it clear that there are no universal marketing answers – under 30 million people in five countries spread across an area the size of Australia.

On the positive side, the cultures are close in kind, as are the languages – except for Finnish; and there is no real problem there either. Finland's business community has long-standing ties with Sweden – the two countries were effectively one for 700 years until the 19th century. More generally, English is widely used in business, sometimes between the Scandinavians themselves, and there are other identifiable characteristics which can help the UK marketing professional.

Business style

Some say that a common Scandinavian feature is an unfashionably collective mentality, a contrast with the more individualistic nature of the English-speaking world. This view is, I believe, mistaken.

Certainly, in business it is a matter of style rather than a basically different approach.

The Scandinavians are, by nature, less confrontational than us. It is not that they insist on consensus in reaching important decisions; far more, they would say, a case of ensuring that all relevant views are properly taken into account. The more forthright Scandinavians might further argue that they have learned not to confuse aggression and determination in their business dealings.

More seriously, the market economy is alive and well in Scandinavia as a whole, but is allied to a keen sense of social justice which can, and does, influence the marketing approach, perhaps most significantly where 'green' or ethical issues are at stake. This certainly underpins the average Swedish customer's regular demand for information, not hype, from the seller in any promotion.

An emphasis on product design and presentation is another common feature. Denmark and Sweden in particular have an established international reputation. This is not accidental, but a marketing response to knowledgeable customer demand. Indeed, most products, even esoteric industrial plant, tend to sell on design as well as function in Nordic markets. Achieving this appreciation of commercial design and presentation is an educative process but customer-led innovation is, arguably, further developed in Scandinavian markets than elsewhere.

The ground rules as we know them apply in advertising, PR and marketing itself. They are all well-established disciplines where the background knowledge of local practitioners, large and small, can be invaluable in getting the business approach right. Nowhere more so than when trying to amuse customers while selling to them. Conventional wisdom once was that sending up the company or its product would make the customer suspicious. The more likely truth was that the organisation believed that the firm and its product or service were no joking matter. Today that is so much history. Unsuccessful humour can, indeed, be dangerous but achieving a reputation for amusing promotional ideas is positively sought after in many sectors.

Scandinavians, too, know that laughing with the customer can be good business. Their approach mirrors that of other similarly developed markets peopled by high disposable incomes. Their humour is best characterised as 'universal European' with, of course, those important local variations. To say 'anything goes' would be an exaggeration, although the Nordic reputation for an endearing frankness in personal matters is, from a British stand-point, well earned.

Competitive edge

So, what will give your offering – physical product or commercial service – a competitive edge in the marketplace? Taking a global approach to the Scandinavians will not do the trick; each country has a strong but healthy sense of national identity. Norway may have been part of Sweden until 1906, but Norwegians prefer not to be mistaken for their immediate neighbours. After all, you would not be thanked for calling a Welshman English, would you?

In short, it is not enough simply to translate your promotional hardware into the local language – demonstrating a real under-standing of the individual market and its custom and practice is essential. The experience of successful companies in Scandinavia shows that there are real rewards for those who go the extra mile in meeting local sensitivities and preferences. As ever, it is a question of ensuring that customers are being offered what they want or need, not just what it is convenient for you to provide.

Checklist

Scandinavians like:

- information, not, hype from the seller in any promotion;
- an emphasis on product design and presentation as well as function;
- organisations with a real understanding of their market, its customs and practices – not just a translation of promotional hardware;
- an understanding of their keen sense of social justice and aware-ness of 'green' and ethical issues;
- ensuring that all relevant views are properly taken into account in decision making;
- suppliers who go the extra mile in meeting local sensitivities and preferences;
- being offered what they want or need, not just what it is con-venient for you to provide;

- customer-led innovation;
- amusing promotional ideas (in the right market);
- trying out their English on you – and for you to try out any Danish, Finnish, Icelandic, Norwegian or Swedish on them.

38

Export Market Development

Laura Black, Euro PA & Associates

Using a consultant

One of the many 'how to do it' books in our office has the famous words 'I'll be there in the morning' at the beginning of one chapter. The consultants at Euro PA can relate to this – Baku, Buenos Aires, Helsinki, Kingston, New York and Sydney have all been on the travel schedule for us this year. All at the bidding of clients who generally give more than 24 hours' notice. But we are ready to go anywhere, anytime to find an export market. How does this help our clients?:

- It saves them a lot of management time and money.
- It gives them a lot of flexibility.
- Best of all, it puts the skills of a professional at their disposal in a very cost-effective way.

Most businesses want to develop their export business but either lack of time or disinclination to travel may hold them back. And it is not every company that can afford a dedicated export marketing specialist on the payroll – particularly in the case of SMEs. Even if they could, it would be difficult to handle all the potential export markets from one desk with one person. Inevitably, markets would be neglected. That is where using a specialist consultancy like Euro PA has significant benefits. Our consultants expect to travel, work on the move, and keep clients and potential customers happy. It needs a special kind of person to do this and some sophisticated management of communications and briefings backwards and forwards across time zones, languages and cultures.

Here is a scenario that many MDs will be familiar with. Domestic sales are going well but there is an opinion in the boardroom that a product or service may have potential sales abroad, or maybe there is interest in making an acquisition or joint venture in a foreign market. But there is no one in the company who knows how to check out the potential markets. One solution is to give the job to a board member reaching retirement who then accumulates a lot of air miles and spends a lot of money visiting all sorts of places on an ad hoc basis. A company might also consult its industry department or its local chamber of commerce. They will probably make some helpful suggestions about country briefings or travel grants for an outward mission to the markets in question. Before you can say 'travellers' cheques' the domestic sales specialist has signed up for a 'mission', booked a flight and hotel and is off to some far-flung place.

There is another way.

Consultancies like Euro PA make their living by helping businesses to find out who the movers and shakers are in key segments of foreign markets. Euro PA works for UK and foreign companies and trade associations, and serves them by having an international network of consultants on its books, many of whom live or have worked overseas, who are known to be trustworthy, are cost effective and interested in repeat business. Furthermore, a consultant may carry briefs for several clients to one country at one time. This makes for savings for individual clients as travel and accommodation costs are shared. Most importantly of all, Euro PA can make good contacts for a client by understanding how a foreign market operates. This increases the chances of success when the client does eventually visit the potential market. No wasted time, no wasted airfare, and no wasted expenses because the groundwork has been done, and there is already an understanding developing between client and potential customer.

Finally, this chapter would not be complete without a reference to the 'cultural differences' that sometimes occur in foreign markets and may be a trap for the unwary exporter. This is typically seen as a British problem, but it also affects foreign nationals as they travel. Euro PA does not try to make potential customers fit in with a stereotype. If potential customers want to drink half the night away (using tiny coffee cups, or even smaller vodka glasses) or talk into the early hours about their family history in their own language, that is fine by us. But we will warn clients of what to expect and we will take some of the pressure out of these 'cultural exchanges'. We are not just there in the morning – we will be there right through the night, too, if it will get a deal for our clients.

Next time a foreign market beckons, remember that it need not be an expensive gamble.

Action checklist for choosing a consultant

The Institute of Management offers the following advice when using a consultancy service:

- Involve senior management from the beginning.
- Gain an awareness of the number and scope of management consulting firms, including their range of services and specialist fields.
- Prepare a shortlist of possible consultants, either from directories/registers or word of mouth. Obtain references from previous clients to establish a consultant's track record.
- Ask for a preliminary written survey from consultants on your shortlist. This should be free, although in certain circumstances a nominal charge may be made.
- Study the consultancy proposals submitted, which should have the following common features:
  - an understanding of the product and potential markets;
  - an indication of the consultant's management style and approach;
  - a programme of work;
  - a timetable to accomplish the work;
  - details of staff involved, including relevant qualifications and experience;
  - the resources required from you, such as time, information and equipment
  - estimates of fees and costs;

- a summary of the results and benefits to be achieved from the project.
- Explain to all concerned why a consultant is being employed and appoint someone as the main contact with the consultant.
- Ask for regular reports on the progress of the assignment. Measure actual progress against the agreed objectives. Ensure that your requirements are not being shrouded by consultant preferences.
- Have a debriefing session before the end of the consultancy. Make sure the consultant summarises the findings and conclusions of the project either in a report or in a presentation. Ensure there are no misunderstandings or errors.
- Assess the effectiveness of the consultancy on completion of the export programme.

39

Nordic Property

The Profi Group (with additional information from Alan Rambi, Rambi and Partners)

Estate agents and the property market

Estate agents operate in the Nordic countries in much the same way as in the UK. If you need to rent or purchase property, the local British embassy will be able to supply you with the names of reputable agents who operate in the areas and types of property in which you are interested. The following rentals and sterling equivalent are based on data and exchange rates available in the second quarter of 1998.

There is a tendency in some markets to use combined office and warehouse premises, which could be attractive to UK exporters.

Other than Denmark, all Nordic countries have their population clustered round a small coastal strip which means that a single local office can cover the whole country. Denmark itself is a very compact country so here again a single office can work well. Ole Christensen of the British Embassy in Copenhagen suggests that Denmark is actually the natural location for a single office to support the whole Nordic region (it is also in a good position to support the Baltic states).

However, for central distribution Alan White, of the British Consulate General in Gothenburg, believes that this will make a good central distribution point for the Scandinavian and Baltic regions as it is the largest port serving both Sweden and Norway as well as being the second largest for Finland. It has a 200 kilometre hinterland containing the bulk of Nordic manufacturing.

In addition to the following rents there is often VAT as well as a property tax of 5–10 per cent.

The property market is governed by a simple and straightforward legal system. In smaller property transactions it is common for the purchaser's or tenant's lawyer simply to check the documentation provided by the landlord's lawyer. Also agents such as the Profi Group, who act for the tenant, can perform this function.

Denmark

Increasing confidence has had some upward effect on Danish rentals. However, they have a historic problem with leases which are very difficult to terminate. New laws are expected which will enable more flexible leases to be used. Because Denmark has a very decentralised economy you could consider setting up a branch office in one of the lower rent areas outside Copenhagen.

Office vacancy rates are about 3–4 per cent in central Copenhagen. Office rentals in central Copenhagen are in the region of DKr1,200 (£105) per m² dropping to about DKr800 in Aarhus (£70).

Finland

Since 1997 the office rental market in Finland has staged a full recovery and vacancy rates in central Helsinki are now 4 per cent. Rentals for the best properties in Helsinki are in the range of FIM1,000 to 1,200 (£110 to £135) per m².

Norway

Oslo was the first Scandinavian capital to be affected by recession in 1988, but it was also the first to start its recovery. Office vacancy rates are in the order of 5 per cent, although this can be as high as 12 per cent in the suburbs. Prime office rents are in the range

NKr1,800 to 2,200 (£145 to £175) per m². Rents in the south and east are substantially lower, although there is a shortage of modern office space in these regions.

Sweden

The strength of the Swedish economic recovery has meant that office space in Stockholm has become very scarce with only about 5 per cent vacancy, as opposed to nearly 20 per cent in the early 1990s. This is of course reflected in the cost of property. Annual rental of Skr2,800 to 3,000 (£200 to £230) per m² prevail in central Stockholm. Considerable savings can be achieved by moving to the suburbs where rents are in the range Skr1,300 to 1,500 (£100 to £115).

Rents drop even further in the provinces. Gothenburg has approximately 9 per cent vacancy and rents are in the band Skr800 to 1,300 (£60 to £100). In Malmo vacancy is approximately 10 per cent and rents Skr750 to 1,200 (£60 to £90).

40

Recruitment in Scandinavia

Jan Johnsson, Morgan and Partners

Background information for successful recruitment

In breaking into a new market, it is essential that you conduct a rigorous research to ensure that you will have the best possible chance of success. Much of this research can be done personally, using publications and government agencies to provide useful background information.

However, there is no substitute for having someone on the ground who can give you guidance as to what you should and should not do. If you want to recruit local personnel, it is essential that you select some local resource to help with that process. Using a UK-based consultancy is unlikely to succeed, since they will probably know less about the new market than you do, although they may know more about your corporate culture than an overseas consultancy.

Ideally, you should work with local intermediaries, who have the ability to evaluate and assimilate your specific market needs, business philosophy and corporate culture quickly. This is not easy for someone who has not already made that 'cultural bridge' themselves.

To be successful in this process, you can work with a recruitment company which understands where you are coming from and what you need to do in Scandinavia and the Nordic countries. To succeed, recognise that whatever you may hear about local similarities, this region is composed of a number of separate cultures and languages. A Finnish person may well not understand a word of a Danish person's language.

Dealing with a large, multinational consultancy is likely to prove frustrating, since they are unlikely to devote the time and effort to 'tailoring' a solution for your unique needs, preferring to fit you into one of their 'off the shelf' numbers. A smaller practice, with a presence in both the UK and Scandinavia, and a well-matched skills set, would probably have a much better chance of success.

Often it is difficult to find high calibre staff through advertising and it is necessary to 'search' for them.

The following points relate to Sweden but other Nordic countries will be very similar:

1. It is very hard for an employer to terminate an employee's employment.
2. We have:
   - a 40-hour working week;
   - 5 weeks' paid holiday;
   - 90 per cent of salary when sick (paid by the state), except for the first two days;
   - retirement with pension when 65 years old. This is based on the state retirement scheme. Many employees will have a private pension scheme to augment this;
   - when having a baby you are allowed to be off work with 90 per cent of your salary for nine months (paid by the state). Your employment cannot be terminated during this time.
3. An employee, for instance a sales representative, employed in one country, say Sweden, can work in another such as Norway.
4. It is common for the employment contract to be in English, especially if you are dealing with international companies.
5. An employee will expect to be able to negotiate an individual contract rather than just accept the employer's standard contract (except maybe for 'blue collar' labour). The contract could include bonus on target earnings, car allowance, company cars, mobile phones etc.

6. Hidden costs can considerably increase employment costs. This will include employer's social security contributions, which can be as high as 35 per cent of employee's gross salary in some Nordic states.

7. Nordic nationals may have to go off for annual military service.

Appendices

Index

References in italic indicate figures or tables

Index of Advertisers